YOUR
FIFTH
YEAR

YOUR FIFTH YEAR

How College Graduates Can Discover and Live Their Dreams

ROBERT G. AZZARITO

A TO Z PRESS - VIRGINIA

Your Fifth Year is printed in 2014 by
Createspace, Inc. located in Charleston, South Carolina

Copyright © 2014 by Robert G. Azzarito

Printed in the United States of America

Library of Congress Cataloging-in-Publication Data

Azzarito, Robert Glenn

pages cm

Your Fifth Year: Helping College Graduates Discover and Live Their Dreams Navigating the Transition to Your Post-College Life/ Robert Azzarito-1st edition

Copy editor: Amy Azzarito

Design: Team 4 Createspace, Inc. A division of Amazon

ISBN-13: 9781482770568
ISBN-10: 1482770563

1. Life-Goals 2. College-graduates 3. Coaching 4. Dreams I. Title

12 1 10 9 8 7 6 5 4 3 2 1

Published in 2014 by A to Z Press
Fredericksburg, VA

AUTHOR'S NOTE

This book is written in honor of the many college students I've had the privilege of working with for over twenty five years. You have shared with me some of your hardest struggles, deepest fears, loftiest dreams, and exhilarating hopes. My life has been enriched, challenged, and motivated as a result of knowing you. I am encouraged about the future of this country and world because I have seen the seeds of change, promise, and innovation within you, the next generation of leaders. I hope this book can help college graduates get moving on the road of finding and living their dreams.

TABLE of CONTENTS

FOREWORD

During my winter break from college in December, 2004, Bob Azzarito took me to Honduras to serve the poor. I was a shy 21-year old student at the time, unsure of what I wanted to do in life and confused as to where I was heading after graduation. I had no sense of direction and lacked the self-confidence to have big dreams.

But in an unexpected way, I discovered my life calling during that trip. And even though everyone else thought that I'd fail, Bob encouraged me to pursue that calling.

Bob has been my life coach and mentor since then, helping me accomplish things that I never imagined were possible. He has brought out this strength in me that I had no idea was there, and has given me the courage to live an extraordinary life after college.

Without his encouragement, I would have never thought I'd have the ability to start a nationally recognized nonprofit organization that would raise millions of dollars to aid the poor in Central America.

Without his inspiring stories and life lessons, I would have never moved down to Honduras where I've had to learn a new language and adapt to a completely different culture.

Without his words of wisdom, I would have never imagined that I'd have the courage to open a children's home for orphaned and vulnerable children in Honduras.

Without his unconditional support, I would have never believed in myself enough to think that I could build schools in dozens of marginalized villages across northern Honduras, and eventually run my own bilingual school.

I never dreamed that I'd be named a CNN Hero and be featured on CNN and Larry King Live.

But thanks to Bob, I did. Many people have stood by my side to help make these accomplishments possible. But nobody has contributed to my success more than Bob.

I certainly had many moments when I was absolutely ready to give up. I would feel beaten up, discouraged, and confused in the face of these challenges that seemed impossible to overcome. And it was during those moments that I'd pick the phone up and call Bob to get his guidance.

It was during those conversations and email exchanges that Bob taught me to face reality, find my rhythm, explore my dreams, take chances, do my job, battle discouragement, practice solitude, confront my fears, and embrace my value.

What he taught me in person is now available for everyone to benefit from, and it is all available in the pages of this book, "Your Fifth Year."

Shin Fujiyama
Founder and CEO
Students Helping Honduras
www.ceciskids.org
2009 CNN Hero

INTRODUCTION

*You are full of potential dreams and desires
that are waiting to be discovered and lived.*

Ben, a recent college graduate, was back in town for a visit. Originally from Massachusetts, his plan after college was to move back home for a short period of time, apply for jobs during the summer, and begin work in his new career sometime in the fall. He had accumulated nearly 100 thousand dollars in student loans, but at the time, he wasn't worried because he had several months after graduation before the payments would begin. Easily enough time, he thought, to find a good salaried job. I knew Ben during his college years and so we met at a nearby coffee shop to catch up.

In January of 2009 I was having a full-fledged panic attack about what I was supposed to do with my life after graduation. Walking across the stage at the ceremony was like walking off a cliff. I had absolutely no plans for the next day.

Amber, 2009

What I heard from him that day is fast becoming a common story among graduates. In the two years since graduation, he'd been busy sending out hundreds of resumes, worked part-time at an area grocery store making $9.25 an hour, and still lived at home without any long-term career prospects. His pay barely allowed him to keep up with his monthly school loan payment of nearly 500 dollars, leaving little for anything else. He was now convinced that he needed to attend graduate school to find a good job, but he couldn't afford more schooling and was rightfully nervous about taking on any more debt. He felt stuck and confused and I could sense his pain and discouragement.

> Getting my college diploma was a huge moment for me and for my family. However, I hadn't given much thought to what I was doing after college. I guess I assumed I'd figure that out later. Well, it's five years later and guess what, I still don't know.
>
> Jeff, 2008

Graduating from college is a big life accomplishment. It has been viewed as a ticket to a bright future full of opportunities and rewards. When a high school student thinks about their life plan, they often imagine no further than attending the best college possible, graduating with good grades in a field of study they enjoy, and then choosing from among the many career options that will be waiting on the other side of the platform. But society has changed over the past several years and life is not working out this smoothly for most.

> I definitely mourned losing the safety bubble of my college community. The world felt full of possibilities, and yet I felt like a scared little kid at the same time. I felt more ungrounded than ever! In college, I felt really solid about myself, and then I suddenly felt really insecure. It also took me awhile to separate what I wanted from what I thought I "should" want.
>
> Rachel, 2011

If you are a recent college graduate, then you know exactly what I am talking about. You may feel that you are leaving college without knowing how to determine what you want to do with your life, let alone how to make it happen. In the following twelve chapters, I will help you face your future with hope and resolve. This book is about discovering the life you desire, one that reflects your true passions and interests and encompasses all aspects of your living including, but not limited to, your choice of a career.

There is no way you can accomplish your dreams if you do not have a way to discover what they are. My focus is on your first year out of college, but this program is for anyone who is ready to become intentional about discovering and living their dreams. Each chapter will present at least one skill you will need to understand and practice in order to move toward the life you desire.

A Surprising Opportunity

We were losing five to four in the bottom half of the ninth inning, runners stood on first and second with two outs and I was up to bat with a chance to win the championship game. The count was one and two. I widened my stance and choked up on the bat as I often did with two strikes. "Protect the plate and make contact," our coaches had drilled into us. The next pitch was low but I swung anyway and hit a foul ball straight back to the screen. The pitch was probably a ball but I'd learned through experience that umpires can't be trusted not to ring you up on a bad pitch. I backed out of the box, reached for some dirt to rub on my hands, glanced momentarily at the third base coach out of habit, and then stepped back up to the plate.

The next pitch was in the dirt but the catcher did a good job smothering the ball preventing the runners from advancing to the next base. It was now two balls and two strikes. Knowing the pitcher would not want the count to go full, I expected the next pitch to be a hittable strike, probably a fast ball.

At nineteen years old, I was in my second season of baseball at Valley College in Burbank, California. Having played most of my life, I chose to attend Valley College because of their outstanding baseball program. I was having a good year. I hit third in the lineup, played third base, and raised my batting average 100 points to .360 from the year before. That spring several college baseball teams were invited to our campus to participate in the annual Easter Baseball Classic. It was a big event with a packed stadium filled with fans, as well as several professional baseball scouts and four-year college coaches.

During this tournament I played some of the best baseball of my life. It was one of those rare moments when everything you have learned and worked for comes together in a flash of convergence. We won four straight games to win the championship. I had eighteen at bats with eleven total hits, including one home run, two triples, four doubles and twelve RBIs. I played flawlessly in the field and won the tournament's Most Valuable Player trophy. Everything felt easy and in sync.

The next pitch traveled to the plate as if in slow motion. My nerves were calm and all doubts vanished. Players talk about these occasional moments when focus is so intense that the baseball looks like a large grapefruit. I hit a line drive to the fence in right center field scoring both runners and we won the game six to five.

A few weeks after our season came to an end, I received a surprising phone call from a baseball scout with the California

Angels. All professional teams hire player development experts who visit high school, college or other amateur baseball games to find players for their respective organizations. Getting noticed by a scout is the first step toward a major league baseball career and the call most young ball players dream about.

"Hello Bob, my name is Mr. Kubski. I am a scout with the California Angels and I watched you play this season. We would like to sign you to a contract before the deadline coming up in a few weeks. We believe you would fit well in our organization and we'd like you to join our single A team in Seaside, CA as soon as your semester is over. Are you interested?"

Professional baseball is organized in four levels and most players begin in single A. If a player does well, they will be moved up to play on the Double-A team, then Triple-A, and finally, the major leagues.

In one of my favorite movies, *Field of Dreams*, one of the characters, Archie Graham, describes the experience of playing one inning in the last game of the season in the big leagues, but never getting the chance to bat: "It was like coming this close to your dreams, and then watching them brush past you like a stranger in a crowd. At the time, you don't think much of it. You know, we just don't recognize the most significant moments of our lives while they're happening."[1]

That movie character was based on the life of Archibald Graham, who played one inning in 1905 and then five days later quit baseball to become a doctor. In the movie, he says that missing the experience of batting in the big leagues was unfortunate, but "the real tragedy would have been to never have become a doctor."

Field of Dreams depicts the complicated way we move forward in life. Saying yes to one avenue is always saying no to a myriad of others at the same time. Unfortunately, we are often unprepared to make these life changing decisions.

As you may have guessed, I said no to Mr. Kubski that night on the phone. I told him that I decided to play baseball at California State University of Northridge (CSUN) and finish my college education, but thanked him for the offer and hung up. Three weeks later I got the same phone call from the Oakland A's and gave them the same answer. Most people who have heard me tell that story think I was crazy. Maybe so. Yet there is absolutely no way to know if the life down that path would have been better than the path I chose. It was an honor to be invited, but should I have said yes to this opportunity and the huge life change it represented simply because it was available? Would the honor of it be enough to provide the kind of life I was looking for?

> When I was trying to figure out what to do after graduation I'd heard that passion was the most important thing in any endeavor. One professor said, "If you have no passion for your work, your efforts will be wasted." But no one helped me discover what that passion was. It was like I was just supposed to know.
>
> **Chris, 2011**

The truth is I didn't know what I wanted to do with my life at that time and had no framework or process in place to figure it out. The opportunity to play professional baseball may have been unique, but feeling uncertain or confused is not. Like the movie character, Archie Graham, I think it would have been great fun to have an "at bat" in the big leagues, but did a baseball career embody the life I wanted for myself? I knew a great deal about this life from many former teammates who were playing for professional teams, but was this life for me?

Making decisions about the future has always been challenging. In the past, a college degree usually did lead to a well-paying job, but this was not necessarily a better environment for discovering dreams. Without a reliable process to assess their true interests and passions, many of my friends ended up working in jobs that didn't really fit or fulfill them. Ben may have felt stuck living at home with his parents without any good job prospects, but many in my generation feel just as stuck in high paying jobs and luxury homes. When there are no available means to determine what you really want to do with your life, or a trustworthy process for making that dream a reality, then feeling stuck is a possibility at any age.

How do you discover your passions, your real life interests, and turn them into a plan? Is it possible to know what you really want to do? Can you choose the future that best fits with your unique qualities and then work to see it materialize? I believe the answer is yes. You can know what you want, and you can take clear guided steps to make that dream a reality.

> After six months of looking I finally found a job that would pay the bills. It was such a relief. But now, after three years on this job I realized that it doesn't reflect anything close to what I'd hoped to be doing with my life. I'm glad to have money, but I feel like I sold out.
>
> Kate, 2004

Soon after graduation, life goals and desires get easily sacrificed on the altar of daily living and necessity. Some end up with great jobs and a few even make a lot of money, but neither of those things alone are accurate indicators of discovering and living one's dreams. Most colleges and universities do not have adequate programs available to help students deal with these after-graduation issues.

For the majority of my life's work, I have served as a spiritual director, counselor, program coordinator, and mentor to college-age young people. I have spent thousands of hours in consultation with students as they struggle to figure out how to move their lives forward in a society that is more complicated and complex than ever before. The good news is, the extended process may allow you to make important discoveries about your life that would be less likely if you moved on as quickly as previous generations. As I will describe in Chapter One, this process of finding your heart's desire is not something that will be accomplished in just a few short months. But it may never happen if you don't know where to start.

When I talk about finding the life of your dreams, I refer to more than a good job that pays well. You have many other hopes and desires that need attention. I have a friend who is in his early fifties and has sacrificed his entire life to build a successful business with a significant income. But he is not happy. His other life goals and interests have been ignored or hidden behind the relentless demand of his job and he is only now beginning to deal with it. His story is not unique.

This book is designed to help you pay attention to your aspirations so you won't wake up somewhere down the road and wonder what happened to your dreams. The time to begin this process is now.

Think of it as **your fifth year**—your transition year. You may have recently received your college diploma, but your education is far from complete.

This next phase of your life is far more individual and unique than earlier stages. My hope is to articulate what I've observed through the years in the lives of graduates, while you fill in the specific details from your own experience. I have watched some recent graduates stay lost and alone for months or even years after graduation and this book is designed to help you avoid that frustrating pitfall. This year does not need to be wasted in the swampland of confusion and ambiguity.

Many of you leaving college are entering into period of life that will feel uncertain and unclear. You are full of enthusiasm and energy, but also some trepidation. Use this information as a guide to help you place your deepest desires and interests at the center of what you are doing in this next phase of your life. This is not a book written *about you*—it is a book written *to you*. There are other books that analyze this new predicament in the growing-up process and they can be helpful, but this book is written, not to study you, but to provide practical daily help for the challenges you are now facing.

The book is divided into four seasons and twelve chapters. These seasons are not specific to any particular month or time of year, but are used as metaphors for the topics covered in the section. You do not, for example, need to wait for summer to read the summer section, and you do not need to take a whole month to work through any of the chapters. But as we will discuss in Chapter One, this transition phase won't happen over a weekend. You will need patience and persistence as you move through the challenges and complexities of the twenty-something period of life. You won't be able to rush it and if you try, you'll become even more frustrated or discouraged.

I suggest you first read through the book quickly to get a feel for the direction and the topics that are covered in the program. Do this to get a bird's eye view of the whole landscape. Then go back to the beginning, review the material again, but this time work through the exercises and activities.

For those wanting more help and support in the process, go to "your fifth year" website (www.yourfifthyear.com) and join the community of learners who are trying to navigate this challenging life stage just like you. There you will find additional activities and resources as well as opportunities to share ideas with others reading through the material.

Do not waste time floundering without direction. These are important and foundational years so don't squander them. If you do not have a viable alternative, my suggestion is simple: **follow this plan**. You must do something about your future and you will be surprised how much can be accomplished if you get busy and take action. It will work if you do the work. This transition into adulthood is more difficult and challenging than ever, but don't use that as an excuse for despair or indecision. Understand what you are up against and then get busy.

> *"All our dreams can come true – if we have the courage to pursue them."*
> — *Walt Disney*

REMEMBER

❖ Finding your dream is not simply about finding a job. This book is about discovering the life you desire, one that reflects your true passions and interests and encompasses all aspects of your living including, but not limited to, your choice of a career.

❖ Use this information as a guide to help you place your deepest desires and interests at the center of what you are doing in this next phase of your life.

❖ You must pay attention to your aspirations so you won't wake up twenty years down the road and wonder what happened to your dreams. The time to begin the process is now.

WINTER
PREPARATION AND ANTICIPATION

In winter, we recognize that something significant has changed. It is possible to confuse spring and summer as trees remain green, sun shines bright, and flowers bloom; or summer and fall with only the subtle shift in leaf color or the slightly cooler evening temperatures. But winter brings its own clarity with barren trees, shorter days, sleet or snow, and darkness.

It is easy to mistake what takes place in the winter. Much of what occurs is below the surface, and so it appears as if nothing happens. But winter is about preparation. Roots burrow deep into the earth for nutrients and water. In fact, the lack of leaves and flowers directs the work underground. In some areas of the world, a short, mild winter is more of a concern than a harsh summer. Without the preparation of winter, the tree cannot sustain the energy needed for new growth and fresh beauty.

Winter is about becoming properly prepared for your future. Chapter One talks about the new cultural landscape awaiting you as you move from graduation to the rest of your life. Big changes have affected our society recently, making this transition to adulthood much more challenging than in the past. It is vital that you understand what these changes are and how they will affect your journey.

In Chapter Two, we discuss the importance of finding a new rhythm to replace the school rhythm that is no longer a part of your life. This refers to the structure of your days, weeks and months that will become the new tempo for your experience. Think of your rhythm as that underground, unseen foundation for the new, after-college life you are starting to build.

Chapter Three of this winter section describes some of the jobs you must do in preparation for the discoveries and decisions you will make about your future. Some of these jobs may feel mundane, but each one will allow you to make good progress toward the life you desire.

Don't neglect the winter. It is the below-the-surface work that will provide for the robust and productive growing season to come.

CHAPTER ONE

FACE A NEW REALITY

Liminiality: The time in life when people often feel lost, uncertain, and unsettled, an in-between time, a searching time, but not wasted time.

Welcome to post-graduate life. New studies in the field of human development indicate that the move into adulthood has dramatically changed in recent years, and it affects all of you. Referred to by many as *"emerging adulthood,"* this new stage begins in college and can often last well into your early thirties.[1] College is no longer the launching pad into a full adulthood, and the transition has never been more challenging or more extended than it has become in recent years.

Stephanie, a recent college graduate, was living at her parent's home trying to figure out what to do with the rest of her life. She called one evening with a growing sense of panic. She had heard me talk about the challenges of the post-graduate life many times but was now beginning to experience the uncomfortable weightlessness of it. She felt short of breath, confused, and anxious about making a terrible mistake with her future.

Liminality is the term I use to describe this dramatic shift in the way young people are growing up today, and what this new experience feels like. It comes from the Latin word *limen*, which literally means "threshold." The word is borrowed from anthropology and particularly the study of social transformation in culture and society. When the renowned anthropologist, Victor Turner, studied rites of passage among the Ndembu of Zambia, he called the transitional period between social states *liminal*, because it operated as a threshold and felt *betwixt and between* for the person moving through the passage. In cultures like the Ndembu, transitions in society are simple, brief, and straightforward. The entire rite of passage might occur in only a few days. But in most western cultures, these transitions can become extended and much more complicated.[2]

Efforts to shorten the experience, make it "go-away," or trivialize it as aberrant behavior will only strengthen the feelings of anxiety and stress for those in the midst of this twenty-something life crisis. Many recent graduates do not know what is happening to them or why they can't "get their feet on the ground." Stephanie expressed more of what she was feeling in an email:

> *I am writing because I have been struck with several thoughts. As of yesterday, it has been one month since I graduated. I have been pondering my future. As I am job searching, I fully recognize I need to know what I want to do as opposed to what I could do. So, my question is, when do I figure out what I want to do? Or, more importantly, how do I figure out what I want to do? I am*

not seeking an answer that will lay out what it is I could do in my field, but maybe some sort of timeline? Or is that wishful thinking as well? Also, I can't help but feel this sense of urgency to want to move. Is that normal? If I were to move, I wouldn't know anyone where I was moving, so why would I? Am I between two worlds of comfort, my family and my friends? Or, am I settling and not expressing the twenty-three-year-old college grad I could be?

An Extended Threshold

In everyday speech, a *threshold* refers to that six to eight inch transition under a doorway that takes you from one room into another. Architects and engineers will spend a considerable amount of time determining the style and design of the thresholds in all buildings, because if the passages leading from one room into another are not appropriate, the whole flow of the structure will feel awkward.

When working properly, thresholds go unnoticed. But when they are irregular, uneven, or extended, they stand out and create both visual and sometimes physical discomfort. Not long ago, a YouTube video that showed dozens of people tripping over a step in a NYC subway stairwell went viral.[3] The video recorded dozens of people stumbling over that one uneven stair even though it was only a half inch higher than the rest. People were not simply clumsy or careless, but something was wrong with the transition. That is why building codes everywhere are very specific about the uniformity in the rise and run of steps.

When transitions such as thresholds or steps are altered in some fashion or not built properly, then people stumble or trip. That is why we often see warning signs such as "uneven walkway," "watch your step," or "ground under repair."

Maybe there should be similar warning signs posted at commencement ceremonies about the road ahead for graduating college students. "Uneven walkway ahead" or "watch your step" could be stamped in red at the bottom of all college diplomas as a metaphorical warning about the challenges of leaving college. Many are stumbling up the stairs or tripping over the threshold because the transition has been altered, and the move into the next stage of life has become much more difficult.

> I honestly expected college to help me decide what I was going to do with my life. But now I'm graduating and it all seems like one big fog. After four years of hard work, and a lot of money, I guess I expected more.
>
> Jennifer 2012

The First Teenagers

If we look back to the late nineteenth century, we see an earlier cultural shift in the way young people were achieving adulthood. Industrialization and compulsory education initiated a life stage known to us now as adolescence.

Adolescence became the word to describe a period that could not be classified as either childhood or adulthood. The words, *adult* and *adolescence*, both stem from the Latin word *adolescere*, meaning "to grow up." The term "teenager" was not used to describe this group until the 1940s. Now this stage is such an accepted part of our adult developmental model that we can hardly imagine a time when it was not considered a primary feature of the growing-up process.

Someday people may express similar surprise over the fact that this liminal period was not always considered a critical aspect of development. We can speculate about the challenge it must have been for parents trying to deal with this "teenager" phenomenon for the first time. When these parents were growing up, age thirteen or fourteen marked the beginning of adulthood. Most got married around sixteen, and by their eighteenth birthday, they were moms and dads. Those parents were now watching their children make these moves much later. Imagine a hypothetical conversation between a husband and wife during the earliest years of this adolescent cultural shift, before the word "teenager" was even in the dictionary.

Husband: "The kid's fifteen and he doesn't want his own farm?"

Wife: "But all the other kids his age don't seem interested either."

Husband: "I don't care what all the other kids are doing. He's lazy! I sent him to the best eighth grade school in the region. I've been supporting him through it all and he is still floundering. Is this the way he shows his gratitude? I have needed his help for the past four years but have willingly gone without it so he could go to school. Now he is fifteen, and what has the sacrifice meant? By the time I was his age I was preparing for marriage and working my own land. What good is all that schooling if he hasn't learned how to support himself?"

Wife: "Well, maybe people are just doing these things later."

Husband: "Well, I don't like it. What is this world coming to, anyway? Next I'll be told he needs to be in school until he's twenty-one."

Wife: "Oh, come now, that will never happen!"

In the early 1900s, when he was only sixteen years old, my grandfather left his family, got on a boat in Naples, Italy, and traveled to the United States. He then landed a job, got married and started a family before he was twenty. He stayed with that company until he was sixty-five, at which point, he retired with a pension that lasted until he died at ninty-five. Your family history is probably filled with similar stories and events.

The move into adulthood will not happen this way for today's graduating college student. What should we call a threshold that has been extended or takes this much time to cross? It becomes a separate room. Many scholars are now beginning to designate the period of the twenties as a distinct life stage altogether, rather than simply a transitional moment.

The parents of today's college students moved into adulthood soon after their college graduation or in their early twenties, but this is not occurring with their children. When college ends for them, adulthood does not immediately begin.

Feeling Energized and Confused
According to the Pew Research Center, in the last decade, there has been a 61% increase in college-educated 18-34 year-olds living back home with their families.[4] Some say that at least 65-70% of this year's graduating class will return home for a period of time.

In a more anecdotal survey, I recently asked a group of fifteen seniors about their plans after graduation and all of them were moving back into their parents' houses. When asked why, they said, "I have no other options at the moment," or "I can't afford to move out on my own at this time."

How are you to navigate this period when there are no models to follow? Just as it must have been for the first generation of teen-agers, twenty-somethings are braving new territory in the development cycle. It would be helpful if more parents, professors, or counselors understood what is happening in today's environment, but many do not. Some might even conclude that these assertions are nothing more than excuses for a generation of young people who don't want to take responsibility for their lives.

This is probably similar to what was said about the first teenagers who delayed growing up and "taking responsibility" until the ripe old age of eighteen. I am sure there were many in that day who never really believed the teenage phenomenon was anything more than a poor excuse for laziness. Some will be tempted to think the same thing about this *liminal* phase. What is needed instead are ways to creatively imagine this life stage in order to provide the necessary structures and supports for those trying to navigate through it.

> I was so excited to be joining Americorps. I finally had something to say when people asked me what I was going to do next year. I loved the experience very much. But when it was over I was definitely no closer to knowing what I wanted to do with my life.
>
> Mike, 2010

For years now, the number of recruits for volunteer organizations such as Teach for America, the Peace Corps, AmeriCorps and many other non-profit groups has been rising steadily. Although I do think college students and graduates are motivated by a desire to make a difference in the world, short-term volunteer programs can also help them deal with the pressures of this unsettling liminal period. It provides a moment of relief from the anxiety of not knowing what to do with the rest of their lives.

Remember how anxious Stephanie was feeling about not knowing what she was going to do next? Listen to her now, several months later, talk about her decision to join the Peace Corps:

> *I am very confident about my decision to do Peace Corps. I had the interview and they tell me I should have my geographic region soon. I am excited about*

the thought of living in another country for two years. I am fully aware it will be a challenge but a challenge I can learn from and benefit from.

This is a huge change from the panicked Stephanie I talked with only a short while back. The short-term volunteer opportunity gave her a plan, and that made a huge difference in her attitude about the future.

Every year, as we approach graduation, I see it on the faces of the seniors. For many of them, cloaked behind their stiff upper lips and optimistic comments, are feelings of uncertainty and fear. Some are moving back home after college, and very few know exactly what they are doing with their immediate future. On top of this, many believe something is definitely wrong with them for not knowing.

As members of this first liminal generation, you may be hiding some of your true feelings because the feelings themselves feel like failure. You have declared a major in college, and may have even professed to have found a career choice, but inside, you are not at all settled. For some of you there is pressure to find a mate, but you feel so unprepared for that step, you avoid even dating. For at least the past ten years, people have been talking to you about what you want to do with your life and you don't really know what to say. Even though it's hard to admit, you are nervous because life is not moving in the straight line you anticipated. You've finished college but the path leading to adulthood is unclear and confusing.

> I always hoped my exit from college would be more graceful. Maybe I'd have a ring on my finger or I'd be off to Europe with friends. But instead it is an epic time of confusion. I'm excited and terrified at the same time. I'm trying to be myself but this transition is weird.
>
> Laci 2013

Many of you grew up with the security of family and possibly demonstrated feats of accomplishment and promise in high school (high GPAs, athletics, club honors, and leadership). You imagined a broad range of possibilities for success and fulfillment. Then upon entering young adulthood, you now find yourself in the midst of great uncertainty, complexity, confusion, and discouragement, wondering if these early promises or dreams were mere illusions or misunderstandings.

The first thing needed, by each of you living through this period of liminality, is to stay calm. Panic will not help you successfully navigate these challenging years. This book is a guide for you. It is not a book of simple answers but rather an invitation into a process that outlines some important skills and thinking patterns that will help you live the life you desire. You are not alone. If you can relate to any of these feelings I've been describing then know that you are in good company. Nothing is wrong with you.

Stay Hopeful and Resolved
In a recent conversation, a graduating senior described her profound frustration that one of the volunteer agencies had wait-listed her for a position next fall. She had been so relieved to know what she was going to be doing for the coming year, and now she was thrust back into feelings of uncertainty.

I asked her if she had any sense of what she wanted to do with her life. She looked almost uncomfortable saying it out loud. Finally she described, with tremendous animation and enthusiasm, a life picture that included owning an apple orchard, producing local cider, and working a farm. She went on for nearly twenty minutes in elaborate detail about how it would feel and what she would be doing day in and day out. But then she made this statement: "I know this will never happen because in order to own a farm or an orchard you have to have a lot of money."

She seemed a little young to be concluding that her dream life was impossible, especially since there are dozens of ways to achieve that kind of life without "having a lot of money." Would she really not give any attention to her heart's desire simply because it didn't feel possible at twenty-two years old? Her dream may not turn out exactly as planned, but what if there was another, equally fulfilling life that would never be discovered if she so easily gave up on her dream as she knew it now?

It is no surprise how many people do not follow their heart's desire because they feel it is out of reach or impossible to achieve. Of course it feels this way—that's why it is called a dream. But too often they give up because they don't realize or understand just how dreams are achieved. They think they have to get lucky, be born into a better family, have more money, or be smarter.

Over the years, I have noticed a common fear among graduating seniors. Despite being full of enthusiasm and energy, many of them also harbor an unsettling anxiety of possibly watching their dreams go by without grasping or living them. Some become so nervous about the future, that they try to stop thinking about dreams altogether.

One important thing about dreams I will say over and over again, and something I wish I had understood better so many years ago: There is more than one possible "right" life for you. Put that up on your bathroom mirror so you can look at it every morning.

You are full of potential dreams and desires that are waiting to be discovered and lived. If you become so hyper-focused on only one potential avenue for your true desires, you will not see all the other amazing opportunities and prospects right before your eyes.

But that doesn't diminish the urgency to develop the necessary skills for recognizing your interests and planning your future. Living any of your dreams, no matter which ones you choose to pursue, takes hard work. It doesn't just happen by luck or good fortune—but it can happen for each of you.

Find Your System

Recently, a friend of mine called to tell me that Arnold Palmer was speaking at a golf course nearby and wondered if I wanted to go. Even those of you who have no interest in golf have surely heard of Arnold Palmer, or at least the "half iced tea and half lemonade" drink mixture, named in his honor. Since I do occasionally play golf, I was eager to see him in person and hear him speak. It was an exciting day to see such a sports legend hit golf balls, tell stories, and answer questions from the crowd.

Toward the end of the program, he spoke about what separated the very good golfers from those who made it as successful tour professionals. Out of thousands of people who are amazing at playing the game of golf, why do only a handful of them ever become consistent winners on the PGA tour? Most people would assume that it was because they were just better players, but in Arnie's opinion, people who won golf tournaments on a regular basis had developed and practiced what he called a "system."

The key, he said, is for players to discover the way they play best, and play that way, day in and day out. Arnie defined a "system" as an approach to playing the game of golf that was unique and personal to each player. Because no two people play golf in quite the same way, consistent winners on the PGA tour discovered a way to be themselves as players on the golf course. In other words, they learned to play their own game.

The reason this is so hard to do, he said, is because no one can actually teach you that system. Others may teach you a perfect swing, or how to hit the right shots, but only the players themselves can figure out their system; one that allows them to make the subtle decisions throughout a tournament to be consistently successful.

As I drove home later, I couldn't stop thinking about his words. And the more I thought about it, the more convinced I became that his point had application beyond the game of golf.

This liminal period I'm describing can often leave you feeling lost, uncertain, and unsettled. It is an in-between time when you are no longer an adolescent but also not yet fully adult. It is a searching time, which can feel like limbo or like you're suspended in mid-air. But it is not wasted time. It is a time of discovery and exploration, and in the words of Arnold Palmer, a time to figure out and practice your system.

Like golf, it is a system unique to you. You can learn a lot from other people and books, but this personal system of living cannot be passed on to you from anyone else. It is something you must learn for yourself.

This personal approach develops throughout our lives, and this liminal period presents a unique opportunity to get a head start on the challenge. During liminality, you have an extended period of freedom to learn to live in a way that is distinct from everyone else. There are so many subtle aspects to our lives, requiring hundreds of big and small decisions.

We are at our best when we discern our individual and personal way to navigate these complexities and build the future we desire.

We do this first by respecting this period of life as significant and important. These are not throw-away years. Life doesn't begin only when things settle down or you get some direction for your future or find a job. This amazing opportunity to discover the way you tick and your approach to the challenging situations that come into your life is easy to dismiss or undervalue. Again, just like golf, no two people are set up to handle each challenge in quite the same way. Your way will be effective and successful for you.

It does not mean you stop listening to good advice. However, good advice can only get you so far. It can never give you the personal understanding and "feel" that can only come through your own observation, exploration, and courage.

We grow up trying to please those who are responsible for teaching us the fundamentals of life—our parents, coaches, teachers, relatives, etc. Then we try to please our friends in order to gain a feeling of security, acceptance, and confidence. But eventually we will need to become motivated by a desire to learn what makes our life work for us.

This book is an effort to help you find your system; one that is truly yours and that works for your particular interests, abilities, and unique mixture of strengths and weaknesses. Be patient and persevere, knowing that this process is not a quick one. Most of you who have recently graduated from college may have no idea what you want to do with your lives. That is not a sign of failure but rather the beginning of an amazing adventure of discovery and exploration.

Understanding this new social reality is an important beginning. Realize that it is taking longer for all the details of an adult life to materialize. The goal is to avoid letting go of the dreams you may have had for years, and learn instead how to expand on them, deepen them, and make them a reality.

REMEMBER

❖ Liminality refers to the extended transition experienced by today's twenty-somethings as they move into adulthood.

❖ Sometimes the feelings associated with this extended transition feel like failure simply because life is not moving in the straight line you expected.

❖ You are not alone.

❖ Liminality is not a wasted time, it is a time of discovery and a time to determine and practice your system.

❖ Life doesn't begin only when only when things settle down or you get some direction for your future or find a job. It begins now.

❖ Most of you who have recently graduated from college may have no idea what you want to do with your lives. That is not a sign of failure but rather the beginning of an amazing adventure of discovery and exploration.

CHAPTER TWO

FIND YOUR RHYTHM

You do not need to live this year simply waiting for the stars to line up and for opportunities to come your way. You can take action immediately and be a part of the process of discovery.

In the late 90's, there was a popular movie called *The Truman Show*.[1] In it, Jim Carey plays an insurance adjuster/salesman whose entire life, unbeknownst to him, is televised. His town, his house, his entire life is played out on a huge set with actors, hidden cameras, and stage hands. Some might say Truman has real freedom to talk to whomever he wants, eat whatever he wants, go fishing, play golf, or ride a bike. Truman does have freedom, but only within a limited sphere of possibility. In fact, as you watched the movie, you probably thought of him more as a prisoner.

The climax of the movie comes when Truman finally suspects that the world he's been living in is contrived and fake. He makes the decision to either find out the truth or die trying. So he sets sail in his boat for what appears to be a horizon, and battles tremendous fear and hardship along the way. Finally his little boat bumps into the outside wall of the TV set, and then he knows—his suspicions are confirmed—he's been living in an artificial world. So, as rain pours down upon his head, he struggles to find a door that leads to a world outside the dome. Is there more to life than what he has known?

Cristof, the creator and director of the show, breaks protocol and talks to Truman, seemingly from the sky, warning him against leaving his home where he has been safe and secure his whole life. As Truman reaches the door, he stands contemplating his next move, and the risk involved in walking out. The movie ends with him turning toward the voice in the sky, and at the same time to all those watching live on TV, saying once again his often repeated line, "In case I don't see you—good afternoon, good evening, and good night." With that, he steps through the door and he is out.

Let's think about Truman's first few days outside the walls of the TV set, the place he had lived since birth. What will that be like for him? Confused, scared, excited, and unnerved are a few of the emotions he may feel.

Like Truman, you have just left the familiar world of academics. You came to the end of the prescribed journey and someone opened the door and ushered you out, handing you your release form (diploma) and closed the door behind you. The company has downsized, making room for a younger generation of employees. You've been put out to pasture. It is not the same as the nearly effortless move from sophomore to junior or junior to senior. It will not feel like that at all.

No one will tell you what you must do come the first of September, except maybe begin paying on your student loans. There will be no list of classes, no books assigned, no cafeteria hours, no clubs seeking your enrollment, no advisors to meet with to discuss your course of study, no tests, grades, papers, or school activities.

Nothing.

The Security of School
One of the biggest losses will be your rhythm. The categories of freshman, sophomore, junior, senior, defined you and marked your forward movement through life. Your major gave you an identity and a place. You worked for recognition and perhaps won honors. All those sign posts are now gone. The ordered world you have lived in since you were five years old has now come to an end.

The school schedule has been the most consistent rhythm in your life. Your parents may have moved, changed jobs, or even split up, but the rhythm of school has stayed consistent and reliable. You have come to count on it for support and comfort. That doesn't necessarily mean you enjoyed school, but it gave you an identity and a consistency. As difficult as it may be, take a moment and accept the fact that this environment is now gone.

Unfortunately, little happens during your last year in school to prepare you for this transition. Occasionally, you may get the foreboding question from a parent or relative, "So, what are you going to do next year?" You develop standard responses and then find skillful ways to change the subject. But in the end, you dread the topic because you have no idea what you're going to do.

So remember to breathe and give yourself a break, even if no one else will. You're entering a dramatic life transition and it will take some time to get adjusted. Almost everything that provided you with stability and security, direction and goals, friends and mentors, is now gone. Left in its place is a big vacuum called "the rest of your life." Most people don't like to think about it this way, but this is what has happened to you, and you don't need to go through it alone. It is also an exciting time when you can make your own choices about where you will go and what you will do. This book will provide some guidance and resources to help ease you into this new world.

A Blank Slate

So what do I mean by rhythm? I mean a routine to take the place of coming back to school at the end of August, starting a new semester, selecting classes in your major, receiving the syllabus for the next fifteen weeks, going to the cafeteria to eat, seeing old friends in the halls, etc. Now you wake up in your old room or new one and it's the first of September. Everyone else is back at school but you are home or going to work...alone.

> For as long as I can remember my life was dictated by my school schedule. It was nine months in school then three months off. After graduation I started a 40 hour per week job and all that changed. I feel like I just boarded a train with no known stops. It was a terrifying constricting feeling.
>
> **Victoria, 2011**

It would be foolish to think that this is not a difficult adjustment. Because you're in your early twenties, you may be able to hide behind a future yet to be revealed. So recognize that your rhythm will no longer be given to you; you must provide it for yourself. Some people go through the rest of their lives never doing this most basic work. They will sometimes find it in a job and settle into the new rhythm of nine to five, weekly meetings with the boss or team, weekends, a two-week vacation, and a two-day Christmas holiday. But this is still not a rhythm of your own choosing. There is so much more needed right now if you are hoping to find the life you desire. Besides getting a job, you have the opportunity to create a rhythm designed to help you discover what is meaningful to you.

There is a larger story about rhythm. Our lives are shaped by rhythms whether we are aware of it or not. The rhythm of the twenty-four-hour day, the seven-day week, the 365-day year, the four seasons, and other rhythm cycles help order our days and our lives. We take these given rhythms and fill in the details with specifics and schedules that are unique to each of our circumstances.

The farmer is on a rhythm which mirrors the rhythm of his crop or herd. The factory worker, the athlete, the journalist, the mother, or student—each has a specific rhythm. So don't underestimate the importance or necessity of your practice this month. Beginning to develop your own routine will be the beginning of your new after-college life.

Finding a rhythm is the preliminary step to clarifying your dream. You must plan your rhythm so you will have the structure to plan your life. When you were in school, your day usually began when your first class started, or you had a paper to write by the afternoon, or you were meeting some people for lunch. The school calendar determined your rhythm. These demands no longer exist and you will be completely in charge of your schedule for the first time. So let's get started.

Sleep: When and How Much?

What time do you want to wake up in the morning and what time do you want to go to bed? This simple beginning will help you get started building a routine that will give you the structure for everything you want to work on in your life. When you have no classes to attend, no papers due, or cafeteria times to work around, you need to start somewhere. And sleep is a reality in everyone's life. College can make us lazy about our rhythm. We do not need to answer these questions in college because the academic life answers them for us. We wake up in time to get to our first class or in time to review for the quiz or finish the paper. We go to bed when we're finally exhausted, or have an early class or when nothing else is going on.

> I was so happy to know I didn't need to ever attend classes again. I was free from school. Free from papers, tests, and grades. But then I realized how unprepared I was for this freedom. Nobody told me what to do or where to be. I felt lost.
>
> Matthew, 2010

By being intentional about your schedule and involved in ordering the simple parts of your day, you will become more focused about all the other aspects of your life as well. Thinking about a life rhythm is a way to begin taking charge of your life. Don't worry about whether you can do it consistently at this point. It will take some practice but it will be well worth it.

I suggest you make the decision to wake up early. There may be some exceptions, but for most, starting early is much more productive than working late and sleeping in. I'll let you do your own research if you need proof, but it is a fact that people who wake up early are generally more focused and efficient. Christopher Randler, a biology professor at the University of

Education in Heidelberg, Germany reported, that early birds are more proactive and more productive than night owls.[2] When you read the stories of most successful people, a great majority begin their work day early.

> *"A person who has not done one half his day's work by ten o'clock, runs a chance of leaving the other half undone."*
>
> — *Emily Brontë*

One simple way to do this is to first decide what time you would like to get up in the morning compared to when you get up now. Let's say you want to get up at 6:00 am but now get up at 9:00 am. Begin getting out of bed 10 minutes earlier every two days. In just a little over a month you'll be waking up at 6:00 am and your body will adjust. Be sure you are fitting in eight hours of sleep at the same time or your early rising will make you cranky. You will quickly discover that two hours of work done in the early morning will equal at least four hours in the afternoon or evening.

I feel like I slept through my first 6 months out of college. Deciding to not sleep in every day was the most important decision of the year.

Tom, 2009

This can be adjusted on the weekends if you like, but do not get four hours of sleep on Saturday and Sunday, and then ten hours on Monday. You will make it hard on yourself this way. You want seven or eight hours every night, no matter what and the closer you can get to consistent times the better. Eight hours from 11:00 p.m. to 7:00 a.m. will feel quite different than eight hours from 3:00 a.m. to 11:00 a.m.

Finding your personal Sleep schedule:

Learn your perfect bedtime solution:

1. Determine what your typical wake up time will be.

2. Count back five 90-minute cycles or 7.5 hours. Each sleep cycle on average is 90 minutes long and the average person has five of them per night

3. Set your alarm clock or cell phone to tell you when to go to bed (but remember to reset it for your morning alarm).

4. If you wake up within 10 minutes of your morning alarm after three days of going to bed at your chosen bedtime, you've found your perfect bedtime!

5. If not, and you still need your morning alarm to wake up, then move your bedtime alarm back by 15 minutes every three days until you wake up just before your morning alarm. When you wake up before your morning alarm, you have found your perfect bedtime.

For example:

If you must wake up at 6:30 a.m. every morning, set your bedtime alarm for 11:00 p.m. to remind you to get in bed within the next 15 minutes (some people will set it about 8 hours before wake-up time – 10:30 p.m. – to give them enough time to get ready for bed).

By going to bed at the right time for you, you can avoid sleep deprivation, your hormones will be in balance and your metabolism will run smoothly.

And think – how great would it feel to wake up without that alarm clock?

Michael J. Breus, Ph.D.
The Sleep Doctor™
http://www.thesleepdoctor.com/

What and When to Eat

Next, you are going to make some decisions about food. There will no longer be a cafeteria available to lay out your choices for you. You have the opportunity now to take charge of what and when you will eat. Even if you lived in an apartment while at school, you probably didn't think ahead about food. Deciding between McDonald's, Wendy's or Chipotle is not what I'm talking about. If you don't already know, learn to cook your own food. The internet makes it easy. There are hundreds of cooking sites such as: www.wikihow.com/Cook, www.simplyrecipes.com, www.foodnetwork.com, www.angiessimplecooking.wordpress.com. Go online and teach yourself how to do it.

Become intentional even with the smallest tasks such as when and what to eat. You will hear me say this over and over. Make the decision. It may feel like a small matter, but you will need to practice this habit. You can change it up along the way, but begin simple. Later we can talk about health, diet, exercise, etc., but for now, just pick some times and move on.

You're deciding on a morning routine and having a routine is what establishing a rhythm is about. So get up at 6:00 am, make coffee, tea, cocoa, or nothing. Exercise, shower, dress, eat, read, and be ready at 8:00 am for the day. Although there will be no two rhythms exactly alike, everyone needs one. You will feel imbalanced and lost without it.

EXAMPLE MEAL SCHEDULE
(Do the same for lunch and dinner)

	Monday	Tuesday	Wednesday	Thursday	Friday	Saturday
Breakfast	7 am	7am	7am	7am	7am	8am
	BK 1	BK 2	BK3	BK1	BK2	BK3
Lunch						
Dinner						

BK1 – 2 eggs, 2 bacon, juice, coffee
BK2 – granola, greek yogurt, sliced fruit
BK3 – cereal, milk, protein shake

Begin Your List

The next step in developing a rhythm is to divide your day into segments. Most people who have nine-to-five jobs will divide their day into two segments: the work day and the evening. But if you do not have a job, or you are working part-time with random hours, then filling in your segments is vital in order to bring balance and productivity to your life. Part time work can chop up your day and unless you plan carefully you can easily waste those extra hours. Begin by dividing your day into the basic three time blocks: morning, afternoon, and evening. Even in school you did this with morning classes, afternoon or evening classes. Then you fit in study, eating, exercise, work, time with friends, and other school activities. Your new schedule will have more complex components so this planning is crucial.

The only way to fill in your rhythm is to do exactly what you used to do when you were living your school rhythm. You started with a list. That list included the courses you would need that semester in order to stay on track to graduate. You discovered this list by looking at the catalogue, talking to your advisor, and making choices about your class schedule. Then you added to your list the class assignments, test or quiz dates, readings, etc.

Unfortunately, no catalogue or class syllabus is available to determine what you must do now that you are out of school. Abruptly and shockingly, you have been thrust into a wide-open space in which you see a myriad of roads and possibilities but no directions, destinations, or instructions anywhere. But next to you is a pen and paper upon which you must write your own catalogue, class schedule and assignments. You will immediately feel unprepared for this. Don't worry about that, because one way or another, everyone started out here. And the more aware you are about what is going on, the better chance you have of making the next several years count.

The objective for this fifth year is to be awake to your life, alert to what is happening within you and around you so you can recognize your moments and make good decisions about the road ahead.

So begin with your list. What do you need to do, and want to do? What decisions need to be made? Here are a few things you may want to include as a start:

Your Fifth Year To do List

1. Begin work on clarifying my dreams.

2. Develop a clear plan for this next year.

3. Find a job to make money.

4. Assign chores in your home/household.

5. Stay in touch with friends.

6. Read books on setting goals, dreaming and planning.

7. Determine a budget needed to live on your own.

8. Exercise regularly.

9. Find an apartment and move out.

Continue adding to the list as your year progresses. Each of the items will have a number of other daily tasks that will allow you to accomplish the goal. In order to decide how to use your segments, you need to decide which tasks fit better into which segments. You might find the morning hours most useful for research, writing, thinking, and planning. The afternoon segment might be set aside for running errands, making appointments, doing chores, and getting exercise. The evening hours are often good for relaxing, reading, and being with friends.

This list is not static. It will change regularly, as you complete or alter each item. Too often people just make a list and then set it aside rather than use it as a tool to help them plan their day. From this list, you will choose various specific tasks for each day that will help you accomplish the item on the list.

There are many ways to structure your day; just make sure you do it. Don't let your days just happen. You will be tempted to do this because finally no one is telling you what to do or where to be. Of course this is true, but you will flounder and become frustrated without determining your use of time. There are dozens of organizational tools that you can use. Google has free access to organizational aids such as a calendar, planning lists, and weekly schedule templates. You can email this information to yourself as a daily reminder. If you want to experiment with a fun tool, check out the Action Machine at www.theactionmachine.com. Choose any one of these tools and get busy or just grab a piece of paper and make your own. But begin today.

Creating a routine is a skill that you must develop. It isn't a talent that you are born with. It takes practice for everyone. And this practice is the only way to give your dreams a chance. It is not short bursts of energy but rather sustained daily effort that makes the difference. It is the beginning of your system.

> *"Write it all out at any cost. Writing is thinking. It is more than living, for it is being conscious of living."*
> — *Ann Morrow Lindbergh*

Find a Spot

You need a spot to sit in your home where you can do your work, but preferably not a couch in front of a TV. It will be best if you have a desk in a quiet part of the house. Whether or not you have a job, you will need to decide what times you will be at your desk to plan. Find a rhythm where you are doing this work at a similar time each day or on certain chosen days of the week. How much time you spend at this work station is up to you and will be determined by your to do list.

Initially you might decide to spend three hours at your desk, four days a week. Or if you have a morning job, maybe you will work one hour in the morning and two at night. Do not underestimate what you can accomplish with a 20-minute block of time. Many adjustments can be made along the way as you assess your progress and needs, or as your daily demands change. You may want to find an office space outside your home. One of the best places to do that is at your local library or a book store where tables are available.

What you are doing here is taking your need for a rhythm seriously and accepting responsibility for deciding what your schedule looks like. You can divide your time into categories and work from a list that will be developed throughout this program. By the end of the year you should have a much better sense about where you are heading and what you are doing each day and each week to get there.

> *"Be steady and well-ordered in your life so that you can be fierce and original in your work."*
> — *Gustave Flaubert*

Whatever you do, try to stick to your schedule. It will be challenging when no one is taking attendance or looking over your shoulder. Do not use your work time to look at Facebook or text friends. If you learn to act like your own boss or your own professor, you will discover amazing things about how much of life is under your control and direction. When you need a break, go for a walk around the neighborhood. Sometimes a brisk walk can stimulate your thinking and bring new ideas into your brain. It was Frederick Nietzsche who claimed, "All truly great thoughts are conceived while walking." If you're feeling dull or lethargic, take a brief walk in the sunshine. It will stimulate your serotonin levels, increase your energy, and improve your mood.

You are making a transition from external to internal control. You are moving from others telling you what you must do, to you deciding. Even more crucial than your particular decisions is that you are making them consciously and ahead of time, rather than just in the moment. This is a skill that is learned and needed in order to navigate all aspects of your life from this point forward.

Do not underestimate the importance of this rhythm. Nothing in the rest of this book will be helpful if you skip this step and just sleep until noon, eat when hungry, look for work when you feel like it or are out of money, nap frequently, make decisions when they present themselves, etc. You will become depressed, unproductive, and unmotivated. If this happens, climb out by getting back to the rhythm.

You may sit at your desk at first with nothing pressing to do. Sit there anyway. There are a myriad of things for you to do right now, even though you don't know what they are yet. But without a rhythm and a solid work habit, you will not have the necessary discipline to make your life happen as you desire. So get to your desk. If you get there on time every day, at least fifty percent of the work is already done.

One additional piece of advice about your work space: Be sure to keep it clean. Save ten to fifteen minutes after each work period to straighten up your desk, file papers, and get ready for the next work day. When my work space gets out of hand with clutter, I notice I am less excited to enter the room let alone get work done. Sometimes I need to stop what I'm doing and spend a few hours cleaning, filing, and rearranging. I love Gretchen Rubin's one minute rule. She says any task such as putting the umbrella away, filing a paper, throwing a piece of trash away, or putting your shoes in the closet, that can be done in one minute or less should not be postponed.[3]

Schedule the Non-Urgent

So much can happen if you make planning and thinking a part of your schedule. Do not give up, no matter how much you feel frustrated or discouraged. Some people make the mistake of using all their available time focusing only on the most urgent items on the list. Do not do this. The urgent items are not always the most important. You may be feeling the pressure to find a job in order to start paying some bills. You may have a student loan or a car payment that is coming due and you have no income. No matter how desperate, do not simply focus on the urgent. Every day there should be something on your schedule that moves you toward your dream and not just items that get you through the moment.

You know how to do this because you have already done it in college. You juggled five or six classes a semester, and even though you had a big paper due in one class, you still made time to attend your other classes or prepare for a quiz. You can't ignore the urgent items and they will weigh on you, but sometimes there is no rushing the process. If getting a job is the most urgent item on your list, there will be many things out of your hands. Staring at your phone or computer waiting for a response from a potential employer is not helpful. So, make time each day for the work that is most important to you, not just the most urgent.

> *"Whatever you can do...or dream you can do... begin it."*
>
> — *Goethe*

It All Begins the Night Before

Fifteen minutes before bed is the time to set your schedule for the next day. If we wait until morning, it is often too late and we end up just winging it. This is an important trick that will give you an edge to make each day count. Plus your brain will begin working on the next day's activities even as you sleep.

The Franklin Planner was a tool I used for years to help me stay focused and organized. Hyrum W. Smith, the original developer of the Franklin system says this about planning,

Think about your last ten days, and ask yourself this question: How many minutes a day did I spend formally planning any of those days? Shower time doesn't count, neither does jogging or driving or canoe time, even though these might be wonderful thinking times. I'm talking about a formal planning time where you sit down and consider not only the day's activities but also your values and priorities. If there is anything I could get you to do as a result of reading this book it would be to spend ten to fifteen minutes...planning your day. If I could get you to do that, you'd not only scare yourself, you'd intimidate everyone on your block.[3]

Anne Lamott, one of my favorite authors, wrote a book called *Bird by Bird*. The title comes from a story she tells about the time her brother was trying to write a report on birds that was due the next day.

We were out at our family cabin in Bolinas, and he was at the kitchen table close to tears, surrounded by binder paper and pencils and unopened books on birds, immobilized by the hugeness of the task ahead. Then my father sat down beside him, put his arm around my brothers shoulder, and said, "Bird by bird, buddy. Just take it bird by bird."[4]

You will often feel overwhelmed by the tasks before you especially as you are starting out on the journey of discovering and living your dreams. Bird by bird is good advice for approaching any large project. But the time to decide which birds you're going to tackle that day is the night before. Before bed, look at your list and make a decision what you are going to work on in the morning. From your master list, make a new list from those items for the next day. If you do this, I promise you will sleep more soundly and enjoy your mornings much more fully. It seems like a small thing, but it will have a huge impact on your productivity and peace of mind. Also, if you spend a few minutes writing down what you are thinking about or working on as you finish your day, it will help you get started more quickly when the next work day begins.

On the website there are more exercises and activities designed to help you with developing a solid schedule. Don't be afraid to experiment with various approaches. Don't forget to record your thoughts and ideas on the topic so others can benefit from your discoveries.

You do not need to live this year simply waiting for the stars to line up and for opportunities to come your way. You can be a part of the process today. This can be one of the most important and exciting years of your life as you move from the confines of a school-ordered life to the life you want to be living. This doesn't happen by luck or accident. It happens as you make plans for it to happen.

> *"Inspiration usually comes during work, rather than before it."*
> — *Madeleine L'Engle*

> *"Isaac Asimov wrote and published more than 400 books by typing nonstop from 6 am to noon, every day for forty years."*
> — *Seth Godin*

> *"The more time we spend on planning a project, the less total time is required for it."*
> — *Edwin Bliss*

REMEMBER

❖ Become intentional about the simple parts of your schedule. You will then become more focused about all the other aspects of your life as well.

❖ There are many ways to structure your day; Don't let your days just happen. Make the decision.

❖ Finding a rhythm is preliminary to finding your dream. You must plan your routine so you will have the structure to plan your life.

❖ It is not short bursts of energy but rather sustained effort over time that makes the difference.

❖ If you learn to act like your own boss or your own professor, you will discover amazing things about how much of life is under your control and direction.

❖ Get to your desk. If you get there on time every day, at least 50% of the work is already done.

CHAPTER THREE

DO YOUR JOBS

Realizing that you are both responsible and capable is the best bad news you'll ever hear. It is bad news because it removes all the excuses, and it is great news because it means that finding your dream life is actually within your grasp.

"Go and get your things,' he said. 'Dreams mean work."

— Paulo Coelho

A large part of discovering and living your dreams is the willingness to work hard over a long period of time. It is not magic. Mainly, we think of work as an activity that brings us a paycheck at the end of the week. But as we'll discuss, it is more comprehensive than that. Some of your work responsibilities will focus on your daily living as well as making plans for your future.

If you are living at home, make some decisions about what your day to day jobs will be. Take responsibility for the basic realities of your life and you will form an important habit for everything else you want to do.

> *"The best way to not feel hopeless is to get up and do something. Don't wait for good things to happen to you. If you go out and make some good things happen, you will fill the world with hope, you will fill yourself with hope."*
>
> —*Barack Obama*

Jobs for Everyday Living

Some time ago my wife and I were visiting the home of one of my student's parents. After a few moments of small talk, this student said to us, "Let me show you my room." At which point I said, teasingly, "You mean show us the room in your parents' house where you used to sleep." If you plan to return home for a period of time after college you must make an adjustment to your way of perceiving that move.

Now would be a good time for you to renegotiate your relationship with your parents. Believe me, they have not thought through this situation any more than you have, but someone needs to discuss the elephant in the room (which is you, by the way). Your parents are glad to help out, but they are also conflicted about what happens next, just like you are.

You are making a mistake, and so are your parents, if you simply slip back into the arrangement you had before you left for college. Even if you try to frame it in a positive way, it won't feel right and will undermine your future success. There are many aspects of your life that will revolve around the basic yet challenging aspects of daily living. Your whole life is not simply about finding the right job.

You will receive a great deal of satisfaction from getting to know your everyday responsibilities and fulfilling them. This might include opening and maintaining bank accounts, paying your bills, making a personal budget, contributing to the household chores, participating in food preparation and clean up, and doing your laundry. If you want to learn about working hard, following through, finishing a job, and not giving up, then the place to begin is with these daily tasks.

According to an article in Psychology Today, one of the most important steps one might take toward improving their own happiness level is making their bed. "Bed makers are more likely to like their jobs, own a home, exercise regularly, and feel well rested, whereas non bed-makers hate their jobs, rent apartments, avoid the gym, and wake up tired."[1] Of course correlation does not necessarily prove causation, but you might try your own experiment and see what happens.

> *"True life is lived when tiny changes occur."*
> — *Leo Tolstoy*

Here are a couple of suggestions: Get the ball rolling by paying some rent right away. In a worst case scenario, where you aren't making any money, at least pay twenty-five dollars per month—anything at the beginning. It is better to pay something, even a few dollars, rather than nothing. Begin immediately to view yourself as a renter in your parents' home rather than as a child living back in your old room. Do not ask them if you should do this. Very few parents say yes, even if they should. You must insist and do not take no for an answer.

Give them a check every month for rent. You do not need to hand it to them; in fact, I suggest you do not. They will not like taking it from you even if it is needed. Instead, place it somewhere conspicuous in the house with a note that simply states your decision to pay a certain amount each month for rent. Then place the check there on the first of each month. They will likely talk to you about it and might tell you not to pay for now. But you must insist. This act of paying rent will set up the beginning of a new relationship with your parents. You are declaring, without using words (words won't be enough for this), that you do not see yourself as a dependent child back at home. This also gives your parents the sense that you want to move out and develop your own adult life as soon as possible. Your choice to pay rent will help lower anxiety and uncertainty for everyone, and will do more for your new situation at home than hours of intense conversation.

> I had a difficult time moving back in with my parents. After four years of relative independence, their questions and concerns seemed intrusive to me. I appreciated their help but also wanted to be left alone. I found myself getting angry almost for no reason.
>
> **James, 2010**

Additionally, commit yourself to certain chores and don't wait to be asked. If you eat dinner with the family, then help clean up and not just once in a while. Remember, don't ask if you can help, just pitch in, wash the dishes, clear the table, put food back in the refrigerator, etc. You are a participating adult, not a dependent child. Volunteer to cook on occasion and help often with food preparation, especially if you don't yet have a full-time job. Adopt other jobs: keep your room neat, make your bed, vacuum the house, and clean the bathroom, even if others use it. Pretend this is your house and you are responsible to keep it going.

Daily Living List

Make a list of everything that has needs to happen in order to maintain a household. Choose 3 or 4 of these items today, and start participating. As you notice other items this month, add them to the list and help out with as many as you can. Here are a few items to begin your list.

1. Buy groceries.

2. Pick up the mail and sort it.

3. Do the laundry.

4. Cook meals, clean dishes, plan the menu.

5. General cleaning inside the house and outside. Straighten the garage.

One other thing that will greatly help your relationship with your landlords/parents: start your day early. We already talked about choosing your own rhythm, but while you are at your parents' house, it would be better to get out of bed before 9:00 a.m., particularly if you don't have a full-time job. You are asking for trouble and frustration if you hang out with friends until late at night and then sleep until noon the next day. To do this is to declare to your parents that you are still a teenager and they should continue to treat you as one.

If you want them to treat you like an adult, then you will need to demonstrate that you are not the same as when you left for college. So get up early and get going with your day. You will need the time to work on your plans and dreams anyway, and you will be speaking volumes to your parents at the same time. But even more than that, you will say something to yourself.

You will be declaring that you are ready and willing to work for what you want.

When you do find a paying job, increase the rent and begin to pay an additional amount for utilities and food. Do not ask your parents how much you should pay, just give them what you think you can afford. Remember, if they see you going to expensive concerts, driving for hours regularly to see friends, eating out constantly, buying expensive clothes, and then paying ten dollars per month for rent, they will get annoyed.

A major part of the adjustment after college is realizing just how burdensome life can be when you are responsible for providing everything. Part of the renegotiating process for you and your parents is the understanding and declaration that life is more than play.

If you are from a family with a lot of financial resources, don't take that into consideration when making these decisions. In an effort to be helpful, your parents might be tempted to make your life easier by either giving you money or not allowing you to pay a small portion of your expenses. But understand that this is not a help to you and you must insist on participating financially.

There are many reasons for this, not least of which is your self-perception. You may think you can easily view yourself as a confident adult simply because you are no longer a teenager and completed college. But developing adult instincts and feeling mature requires more than getting older. You can

> When I moved back home it was almost like I never went to college. Everything felt the same, but I wasn't the same. I'm not sure how to deal with these feelings but it is making me depressed.
>
> Jack, 2008

accomplish your dream life in the real world only if you begin to take on the responsibilities of an adult, which means paying your own way, no matter how difficult the challenge may be.

Living your dream is not the road of least resistance. It is, however, the road of greatest fulfillment and satisfaction. It is the road where your true heart's desire fits within the context of the world's greatest needs and opportunities.[2] This road is full of obstacles and detours, and your ability to stay the course will require resolve and persistence. By taking on these adult tasks you become better prepared for this road's many challenges.

> *"We often miss opportunity because it's dressed in overalls and looks like work"*
> — *Thomas A. Edison*

So respectfully and firmly refuse your parents' offer. Occasional help for specific needs is fine, but the arrangement must be different from your days in high school when your parents took care of everything. The longer your parents pay your way, the more difficult it will be for you to find the life you want.

> One of the difficult parts of living at home is people thinking that I've taken the easy way out or that it's what I want to do. But I would love to be on my own right now. I love my parents but it isn't fun being back in my old room.
>
> Carrie, 2012

Your goal should be to get out and live on your own as soon as possible, so begin by paying what you can afford and do so regularly and without fail. If you don't think you can do this, then you will not feel capable of doing all the other things necessary to discover and live your dream. Do not skip over this part, as I find so many tempted to do. It may not seem terribly important in this moment, but without taking this step you will remain confused about the other steps and afraid to face the risky challenges ahead.

Making Money

One of the unfortunate aspects of your college education was that you were not taught about money, especially about how to make it. There are a number of good books that can help you get a remedial education in this process, but for now, you need to get a job. At this point in your life, it doesn't really matter what you do so don't waste time trying to find your dream job. You will need time for other important non-paying jobs, so for now, just work and get paid. Expect that the job might be boring or not in your area of interest, or not even close to the job you were hoping for. But don't worry about that. At this point you're doing it for the money so get at it. It is also easier to get another job if you are already working.

Living your dream is much more than simply finding a great job, and if you are too focused on getting that perfect job right out of college, you may neglect the other important matters necessary to finding the life you want.

Those who have achieved any of their dreams, often did so by doing work unrelated to those dreams. Ray Romano was a bank teller. Michael Dell worked as a dishwasher at a Chinese restaurant. Woopie Goldberg was a beautician at a mortuary. Sean Connery was a milkman. Walt Disney drove an ambulance for the Red Cross during World War I. Danny Devito was a barber. Stephen King was a janitor. Madeline Albright worked in a Jocelyn's Department Store in Denver. Bill Gates served as a Congressional page in the Washington State Capitol.

Here is an exercise for this month. Approach ten people whom you think have good jobs and ask them to tell you about their first jobs. Also ask them what they learned from these jobs and how they got into their present line of work. Use the chart below to record the responses.

	Name	Present job	Early jobs	Life Lessons
Work History Interviews:				
1.				
2.				
3.				
4.				
5.				

> I've worked so hard to find a job. I spend hours searching online for jobs that fit me and my degree. Then I work hard on my resume always adapting it. But I'm not getting any response! I don't know what I'm doing wrong.
>
> Harmony, 2010

Too many graduates sit behind their computer all day filling out job applications and sending out their resumes. Instead, grab the first job you can, begin to make money, and then get busy with all your other important work.

The Changing Economic Climate

There is much you can learn from any job, even if it is not part of your ultimate dream. It's not only about making money. Seth Godin, in his book, *Linchpin*, says that for a hundred years our economy has operated under the take-care-of-you bargain. We were trained to follow directions, be on time, do what we're told, and not stand out, with the understanding that we would be taken care of by the factories that produced the needed goods and services. We were promised a day's wage for a day's work, vacations, health coverage, and a pension for retirement.

Godin says that this take-care-of-you bargain is no longer available to us and yet we have not been educated or informed about how to navigate the alternative. He says, "It's futile to work hard at restoring the take-care-of-you bargain. The bargain is gone, and it's not worth whining about and it's not effective to complain. There's a new bargain now, one that leverages talent and creativity and art more than it rewards obedience."[3]

The other thing that is gone is the old approach for finding security. For years, factories and large companies have provided their employees job security. There was a mutual dedication from employee to employer and vice versa. Not long ago, I served as a Human Resource consultant for a mid-sized manufacturing company, and every person in the organization knew that at any moment they could be eliminated from the payroll when sales dropped or the bottom line sagged. At the same time, the managers knew that one of their employees could get offered a few more dollars to go down the street to work and they'd be gone in two weeks. They had jobs, but they didn't feel secure.

I speak with students every day who hope that they will someday find a company that will hire them and provide them with all the necessities for a secure, happy and fulfilled life. They are sometimes overwhelmed by the black hole of the future because they don't know what the alternative might look like. Consequently they keep polishing their resumes, sending them out, and hoping for good news.

You can have the future you want, but you can no longer look to a company or factory or educational system to give it to you. The process for living your passion and discovering the life you desire is shifting. People talk about certain professions as if there are some that are exempt from this reality but that isn't true any longer. If you are being trained as a doctor or attorney or some other professional, the big firm or hospital can no longer be trusted to provide security and long-term loyalty. Attorneys who graduate and pass the bar discover that their effort to find and keep meaningful work has just begun.[4]

Become a Linchpin

Becoming a linchpin is a mindset. It describes a way to function in the world. It begins by accepting the fact that you must take charge of your life—not a boss, not a professor, not a parent, not a group of friends or educational system—but you. This way of thinking is difficult because it eliminates our tendency and temptation to make excuses or place blame. A linchpin accepts responsibility for his or her own life—not part of the responsibility, but a hundred percent of it.

If you are blaming even a small percentage of your circumstances or situation on someone else, you will lose much of your power to make changes or to make the decisions necessary to move your life forward. You will be forever at someone else's mercy, and as a result, you will not have the motivation or presence of mind to do the necessary work.

So right now, go to a mirror and say to yourself, "I am responsible." And while you're there, say one other thing: "I am capable." It may sound corny, but those two phrases, understood and digested, are all you need to accomplish your life goals.

You need to know that you can do it. But it will be a fight for a while. You will get better at battling the temptation to blame others and avoid solutions, but initially, it will be an all-out war.

You might be working at Starbucks, at a retail clothing store, filing papers in a midsize company, or sweeping floors, but you need to begin to view yourself as in charge of your life and capable of achieving the life you desire.

You can begin to deal with this new social reality with your first job out of college, no matter what it is. Seth Godin defines a linchpin as "becoming indispensable." In school, you learned how to please the boss (your teacher), especially when (and sometimes only when) the boss was looking (or grading). Now you must no longer think *about* the boss. Instead you must think *like* the boss. A linchpin thinks about helping the company, restaurant, gas station, or grocery store become more successful, and works to make it happen.

Remember, no one is trying to get you to work at Starbucks for the rest of your life. But if you happen to get a job there, you can practice becoming indispensable as a Starbucks employee. You will need to do more than simply show up on time, follow directions, keep the boss happy, and not make waves. You will need to find ways to make yourself indispensable. Recently Seth wrote this on his daily blog. It's called "Beyond Showing Up." He says:

> We often run into people who understand their job to be showing up on time to do the work that's assigned. We've moved way beyond that now. Showing up and taking notes isn't your job. Your job is to surprise and delight and to change the agenda. Your job is to escalate, reset expectations and make us delighted that you are part of the team. Showing up is overrated. Necessary, but not nearly sufficient.[5]

A while back, Sue and I were visiting one of our daughters in Los Angeles and we rented a car for the week. Once our trip was over and we were returning the car, we pulled up to the attendant to drop off the vehicle and get to our plane. A young man, in his mid-twenties hustled over to us, looked us in the eye, greeted us and made every attempt to be quick about the check-in process. Immediately, he wanted to know the time of our flight so he could assess how rushed we were. Then he smiled at us, asked if we had a nice visit to his city. All the while, he was working to get us our receipt and move us along to our flight. He didn't hurry us—we felt as though he'd have talked to us all day if we had the time. He was pleasant, considerate, interested, positive, alert, and efficient.

When we walked away from him we both felt happy to have done business with his company. I will certainly try to choose that company the next time I need a car. I've rented dozens of cars over the years and this is the only employee whom I can actually remember. He stood out; he did something he didn't need to do. The boss wasn't looking, but he acted as if he owned the company and was responsible for the company's profitability and reputation. He was on his way to being a linchpin.

In contrast, a few months later I was buying lunch in an airport fast food restaurant where everyone behind the counter looked extremely bored and uninterested. Two employees were engrossed in a conversation about a mutual friend while another was going about her work with her head down, not noticing or making eye contact with any of the customers. The worker at the register was staring off into space waiting for the next patron to come and pay. The customer in front of me was buying a banana, and waited unnecessarily for fifteen minutes behind others who had ordered sandwiches. She could have been brought up to the empty register and paid immediately, but no one seemed to notice.

Apparently the employees in that restaurant did not realize that how they did that job would determine much about what comes next in their lives. I'm sure they thought they were just biding their time, doing a dumb job, while waiting for the "right job" to come along. But that's not how it works anymore. The new world demands that we create the right job by learning how to be a linchpin; becoming indispensable in whatever we are doing or wherever are working at the time. I felt sad for each one of those workers. Not one of them realized that right before their eyes was an opportunity to begin to make their dreams and desires a reality.

So the goal for you in your place of employment is not simply to do your job, or please your boss, or bide your time. No, this is the time to practice being indispensable. Imagine that you own the company, and it is up to you, within the scope of your job, to make your company profitable. If you work with customers, then represent the company in a way that will make them want to come back or buy again. If you are a service company, then go over and above in your attentiveness to your clients. If something needs to be done, do it.

Think of ways you can help the company improve and put them into practice. If you're not allowed to make changes, then submit ideas to the boss for approval. Stay late, come in early, be friendly, smile, get to know your co-workers, help out; don't just do the minimum for your pay. It will make your job far more interesting and enjoyable, and you will be developing skills that will come in handy as you move forward toward the life you want to live.

Other options no longer exist. If you refuse to become a linchpin, you will be left behind. You may have been taught to get a good job and then do what is expected, but that is no longer enough. Now you must stand out, take risks, and do what no one else is doing. Find ways to make yourself indispensable or at least exceptionally helpful at your place of employment. This is needed training to find the life you want.

Creativity and Money

Most graduates after college believe a good resume is the thing that will get them that one good job which will provide the life they are looking for. But after sending out dozens of resumes and job applications, most of them become disappointed with this strategy only a few months down the road. You will have to think differently about moving toward the life you want. New approaches are needed. The future will require that most of us do more than one thing for money. Many of you may need to consider a skilled labor job as part of your plan, one that provides specific training and even the potential of owning your own business. This opportunity has never been more available than it is today. Why not choose a skill to develop that you can use while you are working toward other aspects of your dream?

Remember Ben from the introduction? He is living at home, working at a grocery store making 9.25 per hour with a 100 thousand dollar school loan debt. He does not like his job, but he needs the money. He isn't making nearly enough to even begin moving toward the life he wants. He knows what he wants to do, but he has no workable plan to get there and so he felt stuck.

Earlier that same week I met Shane. Shane did not go to college. He showed up to power wash my house because I answered an ad that was placed on my door several weeks before. I paid him 230 dollars to clean my siding, gutters, and walkways, which was the lowest of three bids. The job took him three hours which means he made 75 dollars an hour. He made as much money in those three hours as Ben makes in three days at the grocery store. Shane also had another full-time job besides the power washing business. I don't think there is necessarily any connection between the fact that Ben graduated college and Shane did not. But one of them was creative about how to make money, and the other felt stuck. Maybe Ben learned to rely too heavily on his college education but Shane, without college, knew he'd have to be creative and resourceful to move his life forward.

I mentioned this idea to Ben as a possible way for him to make more money and get moving with his life plans. I suggested starting a business in his hometown or learning a trade that he could use to make enough money for what he wanted to do next. He stared at me as though I had just recommended that he fly to the moon for the weekend. But the future may require all of us to have more than one source of income as we move toward the life we want. Developing a marketable skill that allows you to make money is something all people should think about as part of their strategy to pursue their passions and desires.

When my friend Jim, who was a college graduate, was first married he was working part time for a local contractor who needed someone to install the doors on the project. Jim needed the money so he decided to bid on the job even though he had never before installed a door. He got the job and, that weekend, he removed all the doors in their apartment and practiced re-hanging them. The job was for thirteen doors and the first door took him all day to install (a skilled carpenter could have easily done all of them in that amount of time). That job ultimately led him to develop a successful construction business but it also could have resulted in a nice part-time job if he so desired. Getting to your dreams may require developing money-making skills in more than one field.

In the past, schools provided many introductory classes in trades such as electricity, wood working, drafting, cooking, auto mechanics, sewing, and many other practical skills. Many years ago these classes were cut from the curriculum in most schools, being viewed as unnecessary and too expensive. I've noticed recently that some school systems are making them available again. That is a good sign. I hope you don't feel that working with your hands or doing common labor jobs is beneath you as a college graduate. If you do, then consider reading Matthew Crawford's book *Shop Class as Soulcraft*.[4] He will convince you that these jobs are anything but anti-intellectual or degrading.

Joe Lamacchia, who has run a successful landscaping company in Newton, MA for twenty-eight years, wrote a book called *Blue Collar & Proud Of It: The All-in-One Resource for Finding Freedom, Financial Success, and Security Outside the Cubicle*.[5] He cites the Bureau of Labor Statistics projections showing that the number of skilled-trades job openings created between 2004 and 2014 will top forty million – more than twice the number of new white-collar jobs the economy is expected to generate over the same period. One positive aspect of learning a trade is that you will not be entirely dependent on a company in order to make money, and that may come in handy at various stages in your life.

While pursuing my life goals, I've sold shoes, delivered propane tanks, tiled floors and shower walls, installed toilets, did finish carpentry, sold Christmas trees, did landscaping, taught marriage and family classes, counselled couples, consulted with businesses, and much more. I would not consider any of the above activities as part of my ultimate life goals, but they were important on the road to what I wanted to do. We all must learn how to feed ourselves.

Strategizing for Your Future

Now that you are taking responsibility for many of the details of daily living, you are in a position to strategize for your future. This is not less important than the work you are doing for money. You will not get paid for this, at least not immediately, but if you ever expect to discover and live your true heart's desire, then you cannot avoid this work. The goal at the end of this process is to know more and more about the life you want to live, and become clearer about what you must do, day by day, to make it a reality.

Remember, finding your dream life and living the life you want is not a matter of luck. You do not need to inherit a vault full of money in order to fulfill your vision. Some people believe that if they could win the lottery, then all their problems would be solved. One needs only to read about lottery winners to discover that this is far from what actually happens.

Living a fulfilling life is not magic. It is the result of daily, regular, disciplined hard work and it is up to you. No one is keeping you from the life you want. In the next chapter we will learn about the process of exploring your dreams and making plans to achieve them.

Realizing that you are both responsible and capable is the best bad news you'll ever hear. It is bad news because it removes all the excuses, and it is great news because it means that finding your dream life is within your grasp.

> *"Witches are naturally nosy," said Miss Tick, standing up. "Well, I must go. I hope we shall meet again. I will give you some free advice, though."*
> *"Will it cost me anything?"*
> *"What? I just said it was free!" said Miss Tick.*

"Yes, but my father said that free advice often turns out to be expensive," said Tiffany.

Miss Tick sniffed. "You could say this advice is priceless," she said, *"Are you listening?"*

"Yes," said Tiffany.

"Good. Now...if you trust in yourself..."

"Yes?"

"...and believe in your dreams..."

"Yes?"

"...and follow your star..." Miss Tick went on.

"Yes?"

"...you'll still be beaten by people who spent their time working hard and learning things and weren't so lazy. Goodbye."

— *Terry Pratchett, The Wee Free Men*

REMEMBER

❖ Living your dream is much more than simply finding a great job. If you are too focused on getting that perfect job right out of college, you may neglect the other important matters necessary to finding the life you want.

❖ Your choice to pay rent will help lower anxiety and uncertainty for everyone, and will do more for your new situation at home than hours of intense conversation.

❖ Living your dream is not an easy road; it is not the road of least resistance. It is, however, the road of greatest fulfillment—where your true heart's desire fits within the context of the world's greatest needs and opportunities.

❖ You will need to do more than simply show up on time, follow directions, keep the boss happy, and not make waves. You must become indispensable.

❖ If you are blaming even a small percentage of your circumstances or situation on someone else, you will lose much of your power to make changes.

SPRING
EXPLORATION AND DECISION

Most people love the beginning of spring. They've become tired of the long, gray, cold winter and are ready for some signs of life. Everything stayed alive through the winter even though there was little evidence of that. Now in spring we begin to notice tiny new buds and green shoots, bringing with it new energy, anticipation and enthusiasm.

It is also a time of decision. If you are planting a new garden, you must decide; tomatoes or cucumbers, carrots or beets? You cannot plant everything, so you must choose. You explore the possibilities, think through the options, and then make a choice.

During college the options were manageable. You made choices among a limited sphere of alternatives. Choosing a major was done from a narrow list of possibilities. You selected classes from the class list, ones that fit into your major and schedule. You chose friends from among your roommates or classmates.

You might choose between two or three professors, trying to select those you knew or heard about. But now the options are no longer limited in this way.

In the next three chapters, we will talk about how to narrow the field among the almost limitless collection of options and possibilities. In Chapter Four, we will discuss the challenge of knowing what you want and how to make a plan to move toward it. That task is not as easy as it might sound since we are filled with more interests and desires than can be pursued in one lifetime. Therefore choices will need to be made among items that are all desirable in one way or another.

Moving beyond broad categories of interest and getting specific about your dreams is what we discuss in Chapter Five. You will need to know where to look for fresh ideas about what is obtainable and available within your areas of interest.

Then in Chapter Six, we will focus on the difficulty of stepping out with confidence and taking action. We will discuss how to be brave and resolved in the face of possible failure or rejection.

If we can avoid the paralysis that can occasionally come from having too many options, springtime will bring new energy and opportunities. Following this plan will help lower your anxiety and bring fresh enthusiasm to this new post-graduation life stage.

CHAPTER FOUR

EXPLORE YOUR DREAMS - MAKE A PLAN

Knowing your dreams and learning to pursue them is the way we live with hope. Hope is the feeling we get when we believe enough in possibility to put our dreams on paper and into a plan.

"In the long run, doing work that's important to you leads to more happiness than doing work that's merely profitable"

— Seth Godin

Angela Brown wanted to sing opera. On her father's advice she got a degree in secretarial science because "you gotta have something to fall back on." Soon after graduation she headed to Indiana University to study with legendary soprano Virginia Zeani.

One day, when Angela was struggling with self-doubt, Zeani told her, "If you want to be the next Aretha Franklin, go do it; you need no more lessons. But if you want to be the best Verdian soprano the world has ever seen, you have to work."

So work she did. Three times she competed in the Metropolitan Opera National Council Auditions. Three times she failed to make the final round in New York. Then in 1997, at age 33, the age limit for sopranos to audition, she gave it one more try. She signed up at the last minute and didn't even practice, figuring: "All they could do was tell me no, and that didn't hurt my feelings anymore."

She won. But making it to New York was just the beginning. It took her three more years to become a Met understudy. But waiting in the wings was fine with her. Finally, her time came. When the featured singer fell ill, Brown earned the chance to sing the lead role in *Aida*. *The New York Times* proclaimed her debut a triumph. Angela Brown, soprano, who had been preparing for 20 years, was declared an "overnight" sensation at age 40.[1]

Angela was living her dream. Early in her life she had discovered what she loved to do, and for the next 20 years she took that passion and acted upon it each day. The truth is, Angela was living her dream long before the world ever took notice.

You might think Angela is an exception but she is not. Every person, including you, has something in their heart they want to do with their lives. Your dream is every bit as important and amazing as Angela's. Our media dominated society has the effect of making "regular" people feel less significant or important simply because they are not noticed. The truth is there are no regular people. Real satisfaction and fulfillment come when you know your dreams, and you work every day toward living them, no matter who is watching.

This chapter will focus on these two important matters—dreams and strategy. The dream is your destination, and the strategy is the road you will use to get there. No one will give you your vision because no one is qualified to know what you really want, besides you.

Avoiding Drift

Gretchen Rubin in her book, *The Happiness Project,* discusses a common life tendency she calls drift.[2] Drift is what happens when we go through life making decisions without really making them. We move forward in our lives not because we have decided to go in a particular direction but because we were carried along in the moment by either circumstances or necessity.

She described her decision to attend law school, not as an aspect of her dreams or life goals, but because it seemed like a good thing to do at the time and would "keep her options open."[3] Becoming intentional about our larger life choices remedies drift. We must learn to accurately assess our desires and make a plan. The decisions we make while drifting are not necessarily mistakes, but we may end up feeling like something is "off" about our life.

Discovering your proclivities and inclinations does take effort and skill. The objective is to apply your energy to projects and plans that that you have thought about ahead of time and that fit with your passions and interests.

> *"Would you tell me, please, which way I ought to go from here?" "That depends a good deal on where you want to get to," said the Cat. "I don't much care where…" said Alice." "Then it doesn't matter which way you go," said the Cat.*
> — *Lewis Carroll, Alice in Wonderland*

Clarifying Your Dream Takes Work

Most of us are unprepared to figure out what we want to do with our lives. In school, we learned how to follow instructions and complete assignments but not how to write our own curriculum or determine our own direction. We did not learn how to think for ourselves or chart our own course but you will need these skills now. You might be afraid that you will choose the wrong thing, but I want to put your mind at ease about this. The only mistake is to not make an effort. If you take action you will discover what you want, as well as what wants you.

There are many potential dreams that are authentic to you, even though there is no way you will have time to live them all. A big part of this discovery is learning to identify the aspirations that resonate with your unique blend of gifts, passions and personality, and then begin to make choices about which ones you will pursue. Parker Palmer, in his powerful book, "Let Your Life Speak," reminds us that as "you tell your life what you intend to do with it, listen for what it intends to do with you." [4]

Every time you make a choice you will leave many other options behind. That is an important part of the process. You may have considered five or six possible majors before choosing yours in college. That was hard enough. What happens now when the possibilities have grown to what feels like several hundred options?

For those of you who have decided to enroll in graduate school, do not avoid this dreaming/planning work. Attending graduate school simply delays the liminal dilemma for another year or two. Some students head to graduate school hoping that more schooling will provide the direction they need. But for most, it will not. Plus it will only address the career dream, and not all the other important categories in your life.

Recently a freshman told me she had her life all planned out. Since I hadn't met many freshmen who felt that way, I was curious to hear more. She said that she was planning to finish her college degree in four years and then head into graduate school for another two years. She paused and I sat quietly waiting for more, but to my surprise, she was finished. I quickly changed the subject to escape the awkward silence. Deciding to go to college and then graduate school is not a life plan. Much more is needed.

Joy decided to move to another part of the country with a friend after graduation. She didn't really know what she wanted to do but had a few ideas about her interests. She found a job in a retirement community because she enjoyed working with seniors. After a couple of years she narrowed down her direction to Occupational Therapy and then researched graduate programs in that field. But even while in this program she continued to work on her life objectives because there were still many choices ahead. Graduate school, as important as it may be for some dreams, does not answer all the important questions about your passions, interests, and life direction.

> I went to graduate school right out of college which made my graduation less stressful. But graduate school is really not like college at all. It's more like a first job, only one you don't get paid for and suddenly ends. Now that I'm finishing my program, the anxiety about my future is back.
>
> Tim, 2008

"If you have to support yourself, you had bloody well better find some way that is going to be interesting. And you don't do that by sitting around."
— *Katharine Hepburn*

Attend Your Own Funeral

Would you be willing to attend your own funeral? Sounds like a shocking question, but if you were guaranteed that you could come back to the present, would you be willing to step inside a time machine and travel to your own memorial service? This exercise might be a bit uncomfortable for some, but it is extremely helpful for discovering your dreams. This isn't meant to be a morbid or depressing approach to the certainty of death, but rather a way to grasp your honest longings and desires for your life.

In this exercise, you will use your imagination to visualize the future. People will gather to pay their respects and a few will have things to say about you. Then someone will read a eulogy. If it could say anything about you, what would you like it to say? Write it out.

This activity will form the beginning of your dreams. You may even choose to write more than one. Right now, do not evaluate these possibilities. Enter into them as potential realities.

Pretend you are ninety-nine years old and your life just ended. What have you done with those years? What do you hope to have done? The more specific you can be, the better the exercise. As you begin to formulate one eulogy, you may lose interest half way through. Do not be afraid to let it go and begin again. Do not limit yourself. This is fantasy and the place where dreams come from.

If thinking about death is just too uncomfortable for you, then imagine instead your one hundredth birthday party and then proceed to do the same thing. What do people say about you in their speeches? This exercise will put you in touch with your values; that which is most important to you.

Money and Fame

Be sure to enter into the exercise far enough for it to be helpful. For example, you might say that at ninety-nine years of age you have amassed a great deal of wealth. You own houses in four different countries, have a private jet in order to visit your many companies, a staff of twenty personal employees, an apartment in downtown Manhattan, several cars, and a large yacht. You made it into the one percent. Or maybe you solved the problem of world hunger and people wrote books about you and a movie was produced about your life.

There is nothing wrong with this as a beginning, but it won't tell you much about what you like to *do* or who you are. Most of the above items are the possible results of what you might do. But what did you do to create these results? Did you study world hunger and become involved in food production or distribution? Were you a scientist or a politician? If owning a business is your dream, what kind of business was it? Were you a business major in school? Do you read business books and enjoy numbers? Or did you write a great screen play and produce a movie? Do you like to write? Did you enroll in acting classes or try out for theater? Do you visit movie sets?

Enter into the details of the dream and be honest about what is important to you. If you want to make a lot of money, be sure to talk about what you did with your life to make that happen. Another way to do this is to ask: What would I love to do with my time if I had a billion dollar trust fund and didn't need to work for money?

Don't forget to include other aspects of life such as marriage, family, friends, hobbies, experiences, travel, volunteerism, etc. Don't limit your dreaming simply to your choice of career because your life is much more than that.

Your Dreams: A Work in Process

You will never be completely finished constructing your dream. As long as you are alive, refining and pursuing your dream will remain an important part of your life. Now is the time to become skilled, not only at how dreams are recognized and chosen, but also how to take steps toward realizing them. This will be one of the most important skills you ever acquire. Too many people do not make this work a conscious part of their daily lives. They are undisciplined and haphazard about the process or they get so busy with daily tasks that it never makes it into their schedule. But this is a mistake. Knowing in specific terms what your ideal life looks like is the biggest part of living the life you want.

> *"Without this playing with fantasy no creative work has ever yet come to birth. The debt we owe to the play of the imagination is incalculable."*
>
> *— Carl Yung*

That is what your fifth year is about; getting started down this exploration/discovery road. These skills are important even though they are not taught in the typical college or university.

Write Your Eulogy

John Smith was born September 14, 1995, in Manassas, Virginia, to Jerry and Diane Smith. He moved to Richmond, Virginia, when he was six years old. His father was an engineer and his mother was a nurse. He has one older brother and two younger sisters. After high school he attended the University of Michigan majoring in electrical engineering because he knew a lot about it from his father. But half way through college he lost interest and switched his major to......(*continue to write the story. Finish what has happened in your life up to this point and let it move into an imagined future*).

_____

_____

_____

_____

_____

_____

_____

So just write. Be crazy—be brave—but do it. No one is looking at this point, so be brutally honest. You will continue to add to this story and refine it throughout the year. Remember, if the eulogy is too creepy for you, then instead of your funeral, picture yourself at your one hundredth birthday party and write the speeches people make when they get up to talk about who you are and what you've accomplished. When you are finished writing, identify the dream categories and put a number next to each one.

I did a similar exercise many years ago and I ended up with four main categories. These represented my values. I wrote about what I wanted for my marriage and family, my work, my hobbies, and my friends. That was it. Four main dream categories represented the four areas most important to me at the time. I have since added a few more categories but this represented the beginning of my future plan.

Now, years later, I wish I could tell you that all these dreams became a reality but they did not, at least not yet. I'll tell you why in a minute.

This year will be about beginning to understand and articulate your interests and getting specific about your dream. I know there are many other things you need to be doing right now, but this is one thing you absolutely cannot afford to leave undone. You must answer the question, "If you could do or be anything, what would that be?"

Tim Ferris, author of *The 4-Hour Work Week* asks it this way, "What would you do if there was no way you could fail?" He encourages his readers to "come up with four dreams that would change it all."[5]

One limitation you might discover is that your knowledge of possibilities may not be very extensive. Remember when you were young and someone asked you what you wanted to do when you grew up and all you could think of was President of the United States, a fireman, or a princess? You will need your imagination for this work. In the next chapter, we will talk about where to look for more options. But whatever you do, get started. At this point in your life there may be many answers to this question. That is fine for now. You will not pursue every avenue of interest, but at least you can become aware of what some of those areas might be.

The Flinch

According to Julien Smith in his book *The Flinch*, the only thing standing between you and the life you are dreaming about is the instinct to give up. "The flinch is the moment when every doubt you've ever had comes back and hits you, hard. It's when your whole body feels tense. It's an instinct that tells you to run. It's a moment of tension that happens in the body and brain, and it stops everything cold."[6]

Throughout this year, you will find good reasons not to pursue the challenges presented in this book, especially this chapter on dreams and strategy. This is because a little voice inside us exists to protect us and keep us safe. We often resist even thinking about possibilities because we are afraid. In later chapters, we will address much more on this impulse to be afraid and quit.

Do you have an allergy? An allergy is your body reacting defensively to something it perceives as a threat but which actually isn't. How this happens is a bit of a mystery, but our bodies are trained to keep us safe, and therefore, we need their reactions and protective instincts. Only sometimes, they don't read the environment accurately. Or maybe these protective instincts have not kept pace with our abilities to handle certain threats or dangers.

The flinch instinct protects us in hostile situations. But it does not always adjust quickly to new environments or circumstances. Flinch is often about self-doubt. We shrink back in order to protect ourselves from embarrassment. I bring it up here to make you aware of one of the biggest obstacles and battles in your fight to create the life you are wanting. It will be a tiny voice in your brain telling you that what you are attempting to do is not possible—that you are not good enough to make it happen—that you can't figure it out or don't have what it takes—or that it is a stupid dream. That voice will tell you anything in order to keep you from possible disappointment or failure.

Living your dream begins with this first step of recognizing what it looks like. As previously mentioned, your dreams will have several categories. Some dreams might be health related like exercise or nutrition, while another might be relational, like friendships, marriage, and family. One category might be geographical, such as where you'd like to live, or another will be experiential, such as places to visit or skills to learn or people to meet. You will obviously have dreams about what you'd like to accomplish in your work. Some dreams will be lifelong projects or goals and others will be short-term.

Most of your dreams will continue to develop and change over time. Some dreams will require a research component because you're unfamiliar with the necessary information to make a good decision. Most of you are probably in your twenties or early thirties, and you will be learning skills that you will hopefully continue to practice throughout your life.

Knowing your interests and dreams, and learning to pursue them is the way we live with hope. Hope is the feeling we get when we believe enough in possibility to put our interests on paper and a plan into action.

Be sure you do not edit your ideas too much at this point. Dreaming will become a regular part of your life because your interests will continue to develop and change. For this first year you will be learning how the process feels. Every week, maybe several times a week, you will visit this dream and add to it or alter it in some way. This does two things: It reminds you that you are making daily choices that affect your direction in life. Where you go and what you do are results of what you choose. Secondly, it will also show you, on a regular basis, what priority you are assigning to pursuing your objectives. You may discover that you have a fairly clear vision for what you want in life, but spend very little time during your days working to achieve it.

Create a Vision Board
Another way to tap into your dreams and unique interests is to create a vision board. This exercise will be especially helpful for those of you who are visual learners. It is also a great activity to do with friends. All you need are magazines (preferably with a lot of pictures), scissors, poster board and glue.

The first step is to flip through the magazines cutting out anything that appeals to you. It is important that you don't overthink it. If you like the image, or the words, cut them out and set them aside. Continue to pass the magazines around for a period of time until each person has a large pile of cut-outs in front of them. Then it's time to begin pasting. Again, trust your instincts; just relax and glue. Let your creativity take over as you place items on your board.

Then it's time for the fun part. Together with your friends, examine your individual boards and talk about them. It is especially enjoyable to listen to others comment about the board you have just assembled. Did you mainly choose photos of outdoor scenes? What does that mean about your particular interests? Are your choices colorful? Did you include pictures with words or just images? What is amazing about this exercise, when you do it with friends, is how unique everyone's board will look in the end. Even though you are all looking at the same magazines, you'll be drawn to very different images that will communicate something special about each person. You can end the evening with a discussion about your individual tastes and desires; what attracts and inspires you. Discovering your distinct interests and bents will help you become specific about what you want in life.

Chip and Dan Heath in their excellent book, *Decisive,* call exercises like this one, "escaping a narrow frame."[7] Some decisions we make do not turn out well simply because our options are too narrow and we have succumbed to what they call the "spotlight effect." We focus so intently on one aspect of an issue that we forget to notice the information or possibilities just off center stage. Getting unstuck might be as simple as allowing your creative energies to operate without too much correction or editing. They suggest the "vanishing options test" which consists first of listing all the possible actions for solving a problem or making a decision. Then pretend that none of those options are possible and come up with one more. Remember, you have dozens of dreams within you that can be right for you. So be courageous and explore.

> *"It takes courage to grow up and turn out to be who you really are."*
> — *e.e. cummings*

Develop a Strategy

Now that your dreams have their beginning, you are ready to order your activities around bringing these dreams to life. Finding the life you want is not a matter of luck, or manipulation, or circumstances. Living any of your dreams is completely and totally a product of what you choose to do.

> *"Planning is bringing the future into the present so that you can do something about it now."*
> — *Alan Lakein*

Dreams do not become real just by being great dreams. They become realities by you moving toward them one step at a time, one day at a time. This is the second part of the challenge and it is not terribly glamorous. In other words, it is simply and profoundly, daily action. No messages from heaven, no angels singing your name, no orchestras playing, or speechless moments. Finding your heart's desire is daily, directed, strategic, and relentless work.

Pause and think about that. Living your dream will not feel the same way it feels sitting there thinking about living it. It won't be a surprise. It will be satisfying and exciting but not miraculous. There will be no applause for taking on the challenge. So don't wait for it. Your desire to follow your passion must come from an inner urge, one that is willing to sacrifice and struggle to reach your goals, with no guarantees or assurances of success. Here's the thing: life is a struggle anyway and no one escapes it, so why not struggle and fight for what you really want?

Your ultimate destination will be determined by what you do each and every day.

Each dream will have a multitude of ways it can be achieved. Extinguish the myth that there is only one way to get somewhere. So don't waste time trying to come up with the perfect plan. A day working and following an imperfect plan is better than two weeks struggling to find the perfect one.

Just get busy. There are hundreds of possible paths, which is why you can afford to be resilient about your dreams. If one path is blocked, then know there are many other roads you can try.

Leonard Schlesinger and Charles Kiefer, authors of the book, *Just Start,* point out that all great entrepreneurs do not wait to have fully completed plans with precise predictions, analysis and timelines before they take action. Here is what they do after they get an idea:

1. Take a small, smart step.

2. Pause to see what they learned.

3. Build that information into what they do next.

A smart step is defined as "an action you take based on the resources you have at hand and never involves more than you can afford to lose, that is, your acceptable loss." They label this creative process, *creaction,* a word they made up for creativity mixed with action. Their point in summary is "don't just think about it...do something."[8]

This is the exact reason why a couple of my dreams never materialized. It was because they never got translated into a daily plan and because of that I failed to take action. Fifteen years ago I wrote, "Write a book for young people in their twenties about life after college." But that objective never made it into a daily or weekly plan and that is the *only* reason it did not happen, until now. The reason I am writing this book now is because, with the help of a good friend, I decided on October 7, 2012 to make a daily plan to write. That's it. That is all you need to understand to make your dreams come to pass.

When it comes to dreams, what doesn't get planned—doesn't happen.

Another dream I had fifteen years ago was to learn to play the piano. We have a piano in our house, and I pass by it every day, but I still don't know how to play and you can guess why. My desire never made it into a daily or weekly plan.

The dream I had for my marriage however was different. When I projected myself to the end of my life, I wanted someone to read in my eulogy, "Bob Azzarito had a great marriage for over sixty years with his wife Sue. They had a deep love for each other and together they formed a bond that was full of life, happiness, friendship and fun." When I wrote that dream, I knew there were some things that I needed to work on because happy and exciting long term marriages don't happen by accident. Some items on the plan weren't easy. One activity was to see a counselor in order to deal with a few issues that I knew could cause problems in our relationship down the road. There were several other parts to the plan such as maintain regular date nights, pursue three common interests this year, enroll in a couples communications seminar, eat dinner together every night, and take at least one couple-weekend vacation every six months. Sue and I continue to add to this list. My dream is becoming a reality not just because it is a great dream or we have a perfect plan, but because we are taking action, day in and day out to make it happen.

You should feel free to adjust your approach, not based solely upon the difficulty of the work, but on your growing sense of what you really want. Your interests will continue to develop throughout your lifetime. But you will not be prepared for this planning aspect if you don't practice it. Directing your own life takes imagination, courage, enthusiasm, persistence, and hard work. You get to choose what you do. Don't be a spectator to your life. Get involved and make a plan.

> *"A journey of a thousand miles begins with a single step."*
>
> — *Lao-tzu*

Practice Planning

Jan Souman and Marc Ernst from the Max Planck Institute in Germany have now presented the first empirical evidence that people really walk in circles when they do not have reliable cues to their walking direction.

Their study examined the walking trajectories of people who walked for several hours in the Sahara desert (Tunisia) and in the Bienwald forest area (Germany). The scientists used the global positioning system (GPS) to record these trajectories. The results showed that participants were only able to keep a straight path when the sun or moon was visible. However, as soon as the sun disappeared behind some clouds, people started to walk in circles without even noticing it.

Marc Ernst, Group Leader at the MPI for Biological Cybernetics, added: "The results from these experiments show that even though people may be convinced that they are walking in a straight line, their perception is not always reliable. More cognitive strategies are necessary to really walk in a straight line. People need to use reliable cues for walking direction in their environment, for example a tower or mountain in the distance, or the position of the sun." In other words, without some future vantage point (i.e. a plan) we will literally walk in circles.[9]

So here is your opportunity to practice the art of making your own dreams come true. Acknowledge that only one person is needed to make that happen, and that person is you. You do not need luck, even though you will have plenty along the way. You do not need to be discouraged by unfortunate circumstances. You will only be limited if you choose to not do the work.

So start simple. Use health and fitness as your first category. Everyone has a body, so everyone makes decisions on how to take care of their body. Let's say you are ten pounds overweight, in your opinion, or you don't have the muscle definition you would like, or feel sluggish and would like to have more energy. Even if you are perfectly content with your body, you will need to think about how to maintain your health in its present state.

What are you going to do every day or every week that reflects your dream for your body and your health? Decide how and when you will eat. Make a decision about exercise. Will you go to a gym, do yoga or join a running club? Take vitamins, avoid soda? Decide. Write it down and look at this plan every morning. Have a dream, make a plan, work the plan, and evaluate the results. Do this over and over again. If the results are not what you'd hoped, then go back to the beginning: affirm the dream, alter the plan, work the new plan, and again, evaluate the results.

The point of this activity is to make sure something reflects this goal each day or week in your life. Dreams are achieved not by thinking really hard about them but by action. Action taken, preferably every day, will move you toward your objective.

You can live your life, and even live it successfully, without doing this work. But what will make you happy at the end? What will bring satisfaction when you look back and consider who you were and what you accomplished with the years you were given? Are you hoping it will just happen? We can easily be fooled along the way with "good enough," or "this is fine," or "I'm okay." We become skilled at avoiding painful thoughts or denying how we honestly feel about the life we are living.

We may even get frustrated by all this talk about dreaming, working, and creating. It feels too hard and so we decide to give up, check out, or float along. Only a view from the end can help shake us out of this melancholy, and snap us out of complacency. No one, when they are in their early twenties or thirties, wants to resign themselves to just getting through the day, or secretly crossing their fingers in hopes of stumbling upon the life they desire.

Many students I've worked with through the years have high hopes and lofty ideals when they graduate from college. But when I talk to them just a few years later, much of the spark has been doused with the waters of reality, urgency, or pain. They don't like to admit it, but the life they are living is far from the life they had envisioned. Believe me, you will feel encouraged when you work every day toward the life you want, even if that work is only a small step forward. Every day that you do something that reflects what is most important to you, will feel like a good day.

When you settle only for the easier road or the possible or the clearly attainable rather than embrace the difficulties and challenges of achieving your dreams, you avoid growing up. That is why you need to regularly take a view from the end. You need to ask yourself, "Is this what I will be proud of when I look back upon my life?" Remember, trying to live your dream and failing will feel much different than not trying. You won't be great at the process at first, but with practice you will improve. So get at it.

> *"If you go to a tree with an ax and take five whacks*
> *at the tree every day, it doesn't matter if it's an oak*
> *or a redwood; eventually the tree has to fall down."*
> — *Jack Canfield*

Willing to Work an Imperfect Plan

Have you ever wondered why some well-known people were able to accomplish so much in their lives? Do you think they were simply blessed with amazing talents in dozens of areas, or maybe they were extremely lucky? I wonder if they just decided where they wanted to go, and went there? What if achieving your dreams really is a skill you can learn?

In the book *Outliers*, Malcolm Gladwell describes an experiment that was carried out at the Berlin Academy of Music. The researchers divided violin students into three categories: the stars, the excellent performers, and the future violin teachers. In the end, the research showed that the number one predictor of which category a violin student would fall into was the number of hours they practiced. The future teachers practiced a total of four thousand hours, the good performers, eight thousand hours, and the stars all practiced a minimum of ten thousand hours. And then Gladwell reveals that, amazingly, there was not one student who had practiced at least ten thousand hours who did not end up in the star category.[10]

Gladwell quotes neurologist, Daniel Levitin: "The emerging picture from such studies is that ten thousand hours of practice is required to achieve the level of mastery associated with being a world-class expert—in anything."[11]

Living your dream is not luck. It is the result of clarity of vision, careful and deliberate planning, daily action, and relentless evaluation. The first step to this whole process is to know what you want. The whole picture won't come together overnight, but it won't EVER come together if you don't do something about it today.

If you do an internet search for "planning and strategizing for your life" you will find over a million entries. The specific technique you use is not important. You can do it with a yellow pad and a pen if you want. Some of the listed programs look fun, but don't take three weeks to figure out a complicated process.

So take one of your dreams and put it at the top of a piece of paper. Now think about what specific steps you would need to take in order to make that dream a reality.

Example: Get in Shape: Lose 10 pounds, eat right, exercise regularly

- Exercise four times a week. Monday 7-8:00 am – 3 mile walk, Wednesday 3:00-4:00 pm – Bike ride, Thursday 12:00-1:00 pm – Swim, Saturday 10:00-10:45 – 2 mile run.

- Plan my meals for the week. Sunday night- 9:00 pm. Plan meals – Review every night before bed.

- Do not eat after 7:00 pm every day. All food put away, re-frigerator and pantry stay shut after 7 pm.

- Buy a scale and weigh myself at the same time every morning.

- Read one book each month on fitness and exercise and work what I read into the plan. Read every evening for 10 minutes before bed.

You can spend weeks looking for the perfect plan to get in shape. But just start doing something and your plan will develop. You can change it up along the way, but don't wait. Act.

> *"The way to get started is to quit talking and begin doing."*
> — *Walt Disney*

> *"We can do anything we want to if we stick to it long enough"*
> — *Helen Keller*

At www.yourfifthyear.com you will find additional activities and exercises to help you in your process of locating and uncovering your dreams and passions. Whatever you do, get started today.

REMEMBER

❖ No one will give you your vision because no one is qualified to know what you really want, except you.

❖ The dream is your destination; the strategy will consist of the roads you will use to get there.

❖ No messages from heaven, no angels singing your name, no orchestras playing, or speechless moments. Finding your heart's desire is daily, directed, strategic, and relentless work.

❖ Your ultimate destination will be determined by what you do each and every day.

❖ One day of work on an imperfect plan is better than three weeks of struggle to find the perfect one.

❖ Every day that you do something that reflects what is most important to you will feel like a good day.

CHAPTER FIVE

LOCATE YOUR RESOURCES

Remember: no one else is you! No one will do it in quite the way you will do it. And the way you will do it will meet a specific need for a group of people that are affected by your approach, your words, and your actions.

"Think left and think right and think low and think high. Oh, the thinks you can think up if only you try!"

— Dr. Seuss

For years, Frank wanted to be a writer but no matter how hard he tried, he had little success. He had been an actor, a traveling salesman, the editor of a small-town newspaper and the publisher of a trade journal on retailing. But what he really loved to do was to write and tell children's stories which he often did for his own children, nieces, nephews and their friends.

"Frank was always the spotlight of fun around the household. Due to the fact that one of his trades was selling fireworks, he always made the Fourth of July memorable. His skyrockets, Roman candles, and fireworks filled the sky, while many people around the neighborhood would gather in front of the house to watch the displays."

Christmas was even more festive. Growing up, he played Santa for the family, hiding behind the drapes and telling stories to his younger siblings. In that day, heavy velvet curtains divided many of the connecting rooms in order to keep the warmth in. Frank and his father would decorate the tree on one side of the curtain in the front parlor, while the children sat on the other side. Frank would tell his Christmas stories, pretending to be Santa, while the children sat in anticipation of the tree being revealed.

On May 7, 1898, He sat on the floor of his home office entertaining a small group of children with one of his many enchanting stories. One of the children asked him for the name the magical land he was describing. He realized he had yet to name the location of his fantasy adventures. As he sat there, pondering the question, his eyes focused on the bottom drawer of the filing cabinet across the room. It was labeled o-z. He turned his head back to the inquisitive child and said, "They were in Oz, the magnificent land of Oz."[2]

Lyman Frank Baum went on to write fourteen Oz books, immortalizing Dorothy, the Scarecrow, the Tin Woodsman, the Lion and the Wizard for generations to come. Many of his earlier life experiences became inspiration for parts of the Oz stories such as the Wizard speaking from behind the curtain or the elaborate fireworks displays. I sometimes wonder if the now famous line, "pay no attention to that man behind the curtain," was first spoken one Christmas to a group of curious children in the front parlor.

Frank was forty years old when the first Oz book was published and up until then, he had never realized that one might write books for children. He wanted to write what he considered "books for adults" until his mother-in-law, an important leader in the Women's Suffrage Movement, suggested he try and put his children's stories into print. He wrote almost apologetically to his sister, "When I was young, I longed to write a great novel that would win me fame. Now that I am getting old, my first book is written to amuse children." Frank Baum had never before considered that this would become his primary gift to the world.

It is difficult to decide on the details of your dream when your exposure to possibilities is so limited. You may simply be unaware of the many opportunities that fit with your passions and talents. Up to this point, most of your resources have been parents, teachers, friends and a small field of experience. These contacts have come from the home in which you were raised or the school where you attended. You may be feeling some insecurity about where to go for help now that the campus is no longer available to you in the same way.

> One of the hardest parts about graduating from college was the fact that people kept talking about all the amazing opportunities that were coming my way. I knew they were out there but I why couldn't I see them?
>
> Bailey, 2006

You need your own resource community that can help you find important information about your interests and desires. No one will hand you a form with choices for you to mark with a number two pencil. The goal of this chapter is to help you develop your own network of resources for these next steps in life. Begin with these six general resource categories: friends, the internet, books, mentors, experiences and counselors.

Friends

Although friends will be the first resource you will likely be drawn to for encouragement in the dreaming process, I have one word of caution. Be careful about indiscriminately sharing your dreams with your friends too early. In fact, the easiest way to become discouraged about what you want to do with your life is to talk about it too soon. Not all of your friends will provide the kind of support you need in the early stages of your work.

When I was in my late twenties, I wanted to try out for the Olympic baseball team. At the time I saw this as a way to practice courage and take risks. I knew the coach of the team and felt fairly certain that I could get a tryout, even though making the team was a long shot.

I had a friend who had competed in the Olympic Games four years earlier, so I thought I'd ask his opinion about my idea. Even speaking to him about it took a tremendous amount of courage. What happened surprised me. He laughed at the idea. He thought it was ridiculous that I would ever think I could make it on the team. I'm sure in his mind he was trying to save me the time and disappointment. It was embarrassing to sit there, having just revealed a fairly important part of myself, and then have someone think it was laughable.

Your desires and vision will feel fragile at first and they need some protection. My friend's response to my idea was just enough of a bucket of cold water to keep me from doing it.

Everyone knows what this feels like. We often deal with our "flinch" by seeking reinforcement and strength from friends. But we need to be extremely careful when we do this. Not all friends have the personal security or insight to understand what is happening when you talk about these lofty ideals for your life. So in the beginning, your conversation with friends needs to be limited until you are sure they understand what's going on.

Among your current friends, determine which ones have the ability to be supportive and understanding. Those that can do this are not necessarily better friends, just the ones who have strong listening skills. You may already have a hunch as to who in your life qualifies. List them below and decide to test out their ability to be encouraging and helpful. Make a commitment to only talk about your dream to these people, especially at first. Don't forget to return the favor and listen to their dreams, if the person is interested.

These friends will be people who know you well, and may help you visualize your future in ways you've never considered before. Sometimes our close friends can see possibilities in us that we can't see in ourselves.

Not long back a good friend of mine suggested I consider making myself available to area businesses as a Human Resources Consultant. We had been meeting regularly to discuss our life plans and interests. For several years, I had worked part-time as a marriage and family therapist helping people deal with tensions and difficulties in their home lives. As a business owner himself he thought that many of these same tensions exist in the workplace and I could use my abilities to help solve problems and resolve worker conflicts. Because business was his world, he saw a possibility for me I had never considered before.

Supportive Friends: List possibilities below and decide on a time to share a part of your dream.

1 _____ Test date: _____ Yes No

2 _____ Test date: _____ Yes No

3 _____ Test date: _____ Yes No

4 _____ Test date: _____ Yes No

Consider starting a discussion group from among your like-minded friends who may want to meet occasionally, listen to each other's dreams, and function as a sounding board for ideas or difficulties. On the website, I will provide some helpful suggestions and materials to get your group started. For others who cannot do this, you may want to join a group that will be organized through the website. It may be scary for you to join one of these groups with people you do not know, but why not? What do you have to lose? If the choice is between being comfortable or discovering direction, isn't the little bit of discomfort worth it? Plus, they will be people that have read this book and are motivated, like you, to discover and live their dreams.

> I miss my friends from college. It is more awkward now having to schedule times to talk. And it's usually only small talk because we're not in touch on a daily basis anymore. I don't have anyone to talk to about what's going on in my life. Especially when I'm not even sure what's going on.
>
> **Amy, 2012**

The Internet
As your dreams develop and you begin to get a sense of what you want, use the Internet to dig deeper for more information, as well as research specific possibilities.

Don't get discouraged when you read about people who are already doing what you want to do. Sometimes it can make you feel like your contribution is not needed. But you need to remember: no one else is you. No one will do it in quite the way you will do it. And the way you will do it will meet a specific need for a group of people that are affected by your approach, your words, and your actions.

Sarah is an equine massage therapist in Crozet, VA. She massages horses for a living. She always loved animals and had developed a sense of her own dream back in college many years before. After being trained in Boulder, CO, she moved to Crozet because it had a large horse culture. The first person she met was a fellow equine massage therapist and learned there were many others. Rather than feeling discouraged by the fact that others were already doing what she wanted to do, she reached out to these colleagues and discovered in many of them a willingness to teach her the ropes. You do not need to find something to do that no one else is doing. If there is a need in the world, there will likely be many people pursuing a similar dream.[3]

We are not in competition with others if we are seeking to live authentically from within. We want to do our part, and we need to know that when we do, we are discovering the true source of our fulfillment and contentment.

Have you ever tuned a stringed instrument? One way to do this is to tune the strings to each other. When a string is out of tune with another string, it vibrates. You can recognize that a string is in tune when this warbling sound lessens and the tone smoothes out. When we are living our lives, pursuing our heart's desire in the particular way that fits us, we also even out and become smooth. When we are trying to be something we are not, or not living authentically, we feel rough or incongruent. We warble. Something is off and we feel it.

A lot of pressure exists to ignore this feeling. We are often told by others that we should be more, have more, and demand more. Or we are told by our inner self-doubt that we are not good enough and should stay in the dark, or safe in our own small space. Finding your spot is difficult and might take some time to locate.

It will also change some over time; it won't be perfect, even as a guitar string is never perfectly in tune. But you keep working at it as part of your life journey. You keep checking it after each song. You are vigilant with this process because a string out of tune can make a perfectly good song sound awful. Expecting too much, too fast, succumbing to pressure or voices from the outside, and taking unwise short cuts are a few of the ways we can get out of tune.

When I played baseball, coaches would say to players up at bat, "Swing within yourself." Although I can't remember anyone ever defining it, we all knew it meant don't swing too fast, or too slow; swing in a way that fits your style and approach to hitting. Don't try too hard or not hard enough. Relax, be yourself, and let the play come to you. Don't shrink back, but also don't charge forward. Find a rhythm that is smooth, deliberate, focused, persistent, and calm. Make your own swing, and you'll be surprised at the sound the bat makes when connecting with the ball.

As you discover relevant websites that help with this task of dream-making and dream-living I hope you will share it with others. Here are a few websites that will be helpful in forming dreams, making plans and living well. You will need to find sites that are more specific to your interests, but these will help you with generalized information and insights regardless of your particular dreams.

1. Seth Godin blog - One of the most helpful websites for grasping what is new in the world of work and life. Seth Godin's books are also helpful, but don't forget to sign up for his free blog post that will come to your email daily (www.sethgodin.com).

2. Zen Habits – This site is about finding simplicity in the daily chaos of our lives. It's about clearing the clutter so we can focus on what's important, create something amazing, and find happiness. It also happens to be one of the top twenty-five blogs and top fifty websites in the world, with about 260,000 subscribers (and more than a million overall readers). Zen Habits features one or two powerful articles a week on simplicity, health and fitness, motivation and inspiration, frugality, family life, happiness, goals, getting great things done, and living in the moment (www.zenhabits.net).

3. Mindtools – Founded by James Manktelow in 1996, this site is dedicated to helping people learn the simple and practical skills necessary to excel in their careers. Primarily directed to business oriented careers, Mindtools can also be helpful for organizational strategy, time management, decision making, problem solving, teamwork, and much more (www.mindtools.com).

4. Four Hour Workweek – Tim Ferris calls his website and blog, "Experiments in Lifestyle Design." Tim is a guru for creative thinking and living. It is hard to summarize what Tim's website and blog are about. You just need

to sample it. He will challenge the way you think about life, money, career, happiness, goals, time, and more. He will stimulate your brain to consider things you've never thought about before. His way of thinking will put what you really want in life to the test (www.fourhour-workweek.com).

5. Life Hacker – Tips, tricks, and downloads for getting things done. A popular blog that will discuss just about any subject that helps you with the practical and the necessary. It is both entertaining and creative (www. lifehacker.com).

Use your browser to discover other websites or blogs that will help you explore your specific interests. You will be exposed to new possibilities through your research that may spark ideas and options never before considered. Make browsing a regular part of your schedule. I guarantee, it will pay off.

Books
Books will help you realize that many other people are on this journey with you. Some people are ahead of you in the process, and their stories can be valuable resources for the road before you. Their books will help you understand what it means to think like an entrepreneur, to take responsibility for your life, and how to stay focused and organized. If you reso-nate with one of the authors, take a look at other books he or she has written, as well as other books they recommend. Get connected to their blog if they have one, or attend a seminar where they are speaking.

I know you have just spent four years in college reading, reading and reading some more. The last thing you may want to do right now is read. But my guess is you were not exposed to the written material necessary for this next stage in your journey. You must take charge of your education in this post-graduation phase.

I will continue to make several reading suggestions throughout this book and more will be listed in the back. These are books on topics that relate to finding the life you want. They will provide ideas to help you get past some common hurdles, but one caution; reading what others have to say on the subject is not the same as doing the hard work of dreaming, planning, and deciding for yourself. Be careful about using good reading material as a way to avoid doing your own work.

Begin by reading at least one book each month corresponding to the chapter topic. First, make a reading list of three possibilities, then go to a book store or online and sample each one (if you have a kindle you can often get a sample of the book sent to you before you buy). Take a look at what other people have said about the books and then decide which one you will read. Either use my suggestions at the back of this book or find others on your own. A good practice is to make a yearly reading list at the end of every year for the next one coming. Don't just pick up the latest book on the market. You may do more reading than this, but decide on your focus, and then find books that address it. One way to find helpful material is to ask your mentors what they are reading.

Yearly Educational Chart:

Month 1 – Facing the New Reality

Book possibilities:

1. Resource: _____

2. Resource: _____

3. Resource: _____

Month 2: Finding Your Rhythm

1. Resource: _____

Mentors

Several years ago I heard a speaker who inspired me with ideas about what I wanted to do with my life. I was already working as a counselor, but I felt my work needed more focus and direction. As he spoke, I began to formulate a vision for the type of help I wanted to provide. What I did next was very important. I wrote him a letter (yes, pre-internet). For the past thirty years, I have stayed in touch with this man mostly through the mail. I keep a number of his letters with me in my planner and read them occasionally for inspiration. He represents someone whose life demonstrates the qualities and insights that connect with my own deepest aspirations and desires.

Finding mentors who inspire you is an important part of your new education. Books can be extremely helpful, but there is no substitute for personal contact with someone in your area of interest. Sometimes this practice of finding mentors is viewed as an aspect of networking. It means finding your people and getting into the communities that are doing what you are interested in doing. Mentors are people whose work corresponds to your interests and desires.

See yourself in the company of people doing what you like to do. What group do you want to be a part of? Who would you like your name attached to? Think about their work and ask yourself if that is the kind of work you want to do. Are you willing to develop the necessary skills to make it happen no matter how long it takes?

There may be several people right around you who fit that description. Have the courage to make a connection. Write a letter. Ask them something about their field. You may be surprised at their willingness to discuss their journey and help you get started. If you come across one or two who are not helpful, don't be discouraged; just move on to someone else.

It was very important for me to stay in contact with two of my mentors from college. I felt alone in grad school and didn't find the support I had while an undergrad. It was hard to find replacements for the people I trusted and who knew me so well.

Beth, 2006

Someone whose work ethic and drive you admire, even if out of your field, can also be very helpful. These people are usually filled with fresh ideas and energy that can help you find direction and inspiration. Meeting with a mentor, even occasionally, can be encouraging, motivating, and insightful.

One of the many books I've enjoyed recently is *Anything You Want,* by Derek Sivers.[4] In the back of his book he invites people to contact him with questions or comments. At the time I was working on this book and had some questions about writing and publishing. So I decided to take him up on his offer.

Here is the email I wrote:

> *Hello Derek,*
>
> *I read your book a while back and finally decided to take you up on the offer to email. My name is Bob Azzarito and I've worked for over 25 years with college students in various parts of the country. Inspired by you, Seth Godin, Steven Pressfield, Michael Ellsberg, Malcolm Gladwell and others, I decided to write a book for students. I have realized over the years how unprepared students feel for the world they are moving into after graduation. So I wrote a book called, "Your Fifth Year," which is designed to be a program for their first year out of college. I've been thinking about getting it published directly through Amazon and avoiding the agent/publishing world altogether. Since most of my intended audience seldom frequent bookstores, I figured why waste the time and money. I just wanted to know if you had any opinion on the Indie publishing route.*
>
> *Thank you for your book and your story. It motivated me to get busy working on one of my dreams.*
>
> *Bob*

A few days later I received a very helpful email from him which was both informative and inspiring. He gave me some excellent advice on self-publishing and encouraged me to keep at it. He invited me to write back anytime and occasionally I'll get updates on what he is doing next in his life and career.

I have contacted people I admire several times throughout my life and rarely did I not receive a gracious and helpful response. There are no extra points for going it alone. So, who in your field of interest would you like to talk with? Stop wishing and take action. I have a folder full of very nice letters from people who inspire me. I treasure these as much as I do the books they have written.

I have also attended conferences or classes taught by people I respect. The money was well spent as an investment in my future. Don't be afraid to make a connection after the meeting and express your appreciation or ask a question. Not all will have the time to talk, but many will be very responsive to your desire to learn. One piece of advice: Don't sign up for conferences simply because of the advertised topic. Rather sign up when there is someone speaking whom you want to hear no matter what the conference topic. Do your homework first and you will use your time and money more wisely.

Remember my conversation with the student who wanted to own an apple orchard? For years her summer job had been working in an orchard selling peaches, apples, and cider. I asked her if she had ever asked the owners what it was like to run their business or how they got started in the work. She said no. The way to get the needed information for your own plan is to talk with others who have done similar things. Your path or approach may differ, but you will be surprised how often these conversations will provide ideas and insights for your own journey.

For any dream or goal you have, you can find people who are in the field and reach out to them. It is a vital aspect of knowing what steps are necessary in order to make your dream a reality.

List three people who are working in your field of interest that might serve as temporary mentors. Decide when and how you will make contact with them.

1. _____

   Date to contact: _____

   How to contact: _____ email _____ mail _____ call

2. _____

3. _____

Experiences

After graduation, Jack had no idea what he wanted to do with his life, so he signed up to do a year volunteer program in Louisiana. His job was to help with the Katrina rebuilding effort, while at the same time, hoped he would get some insight about his future. He enjoyed the job so much, he considered staying on for a second year. He was among the few who had some building experience and quickly became a leader in organizing the effort.

His decision to forego a second year in the program immediately thrust him into a quandary about what was next. As he looked back on his year in New Orleans, he realized that doing the construction work was a big part of his enjoyment. After considering a variety of options, he took a risk and started a remodeling business. It wasn't the safest choice, but definitely the one that promised the most potential and fulfillment. He is

> When I got out of college, I felt like doing something adventurous. So, I volunteered on an organic farm out in Colorado for five weeks. It was one of the richest mini-adventures I've ever had!
>
> Amy, 2011

now running his own small construction company in Northern Virginia and he loves owning his own business.

Many recent college graduates often look for an experience that might help them sift through their options or at least provide some inspiration or ideas. Occasionally those experiences include travel or possibly an internship. Seeking an eye-opening experience is often behind much of the interest in short term volunteer service programs. The hope is that these experiences will produce a new sense of understanding about personal tastes, talents, and desires.

Shin was a sophomore in college when he joined our campus group for a week-long service trip to Honduras. While there, I watched him become deeply moved and motivated by the needs of the children, especially the orphans. When he came back to college, he decided to act on this interest. He began working in the cafeteria on campus and sending his few extra dollars to a Honduran orphanage. He saved his money and returned to Honduras later that same year.

He told his friends about what he saw and how they could become a part of the effort. During the summer, he organized work trips where other interested students could travel with him. Later that year, he and his sister decided to start an organization dedicated to helping children in Honduras called Students Helping Honduras.

Today, nearly nine years later, Shin lives in Honduras full time. He and SHH built a new village for poor families near El Progreso called Villa Soleada, started an orphanage, and a bilingual school. Each year they also build or refurbish three or four village schools. Shin continues to run Students Helping Honduras with campus clubs in over 50 colleges and universities across the country. He brings more than 700 college students to Honduras each year to help with needy children and families. He has spoken hundreds of times on campuses, churches, and civic organizations about the work his organization is doing in Central America. He was also honored by being featured on Larry King Live as a CNN hero.

Being willing to explore possibilities through new experiences is a way to expand your horizons. Sometimes, whole new areas of interest can open up through a short term experience of some kind. Now is the time for you to take advantage of these opportunities, especially when you're not sure about what you want to do next.

These new adventures can also give you courage to take brave steps toward the future you desire. This isn't the only way to gain exposure and inspiration, but many people find new avenues and options they never knew existed before.

Plan an experience

Identify at least three experiences for this coming year. Choose one of these and list five specific actions you would need to take this month to make this experience happen. Later, add dates and times for each action if applicable. Example:

Experience: Take a week out of my summer and serve in a relief organization for needy families.

Step 1: Research possible opportunities online. Evaluate specific requirements and choose one to pursue.

Step 2: Decide if you would travel alone or with a friend. Contact possible friends who may want to go.

Step 3: Decide on the time of year you would like to go and possible dates.

Step 4: Determine your form of travel and plan the itinerary.

Step 5: Make contact with the organization and ask for more details.

Counselors

Courteney is a graduate from James Madison University and majored in forensic psychology. After college she toyed with law school, personal training, marine biology, and fashion buying. She says she went in fifteen different directions in the two or three years out of college. After several years of bouncing around from one thing to the next she decided to see a career counselor. The results of the counseling process were life changing for her. Through the conversation and many tests, the counselor suggested Courteney explore journalism, a possibility she had never considered before.

In an interview by *C-Ville*, a Charlottesville newspaper, she commented that loving to write did not turn out to be the most necessary quality for journalism. Rather nosiness, intense curiosity, and the need to know, were the assets most vital in a reporter. In Courteney's case, a career counselor helped her see something she would never have noticed on her own. She says it was often an uphill battle but she immediately felt comfortable and at home among other journalists. Now nearly seventeen years later, she is chief editor at the *Hook*, a successful Charlottesville weekly. 5

Sometimes we need professional help. Almost everyone I know needed to get help from a professional counselor at some point in their lives. Thankfully, the stigma about doing this doesn't exist much anymore. A good counselor won't tell you exactly what to do, but can help you clarify your true interests, desires, capabilities and potential roadblocks. The best counselors ask good questions, listen well, and provide great feedback on what they hear.

Years ago, when I was leaving a job and not sure what my next step should be, I took the opportunity to visit a career counselor. It was a process that lasted several hours over a three-week period. I took a few tests, talked with trained professionals, and filled out several personal surveys. During the feedback session, I learned many significant things about myself, and made some important decisions about my future. As part of the process, I was able to reflect on a few past experiences and see how they were preventing me from moving forward in a positive way. Seeing your past through the eyes of a counselor may help you resolve issues that could be holding you back.

Talking with a counselor can be helpful when trying to wade through a variety of confusing options and conflicting feelings. Having served for many years in this capacity with students, I've noticed that people are helped simply by the opportunity to express their frustrations and concerns in a safe environment. They need to know that they are not odd or defective. They come seeking answers and usually leave with the reassurance that they are indeed not alone and the trajectory of their lives is normal. Scott Peck begins his famous book, "The Road Less Traveled," with these three insightful and direct words: "Life is difficult."[6] When we feel overwhelmed, confused, fearful or lost, we need to hear someone say: "You're not strange, sometimes life is just difficult."

A list of Master Career Counselors and Master Career Development Professionals in your state can be accessed at the Web site of the NCDA (National Career Development Association). www.ncda.org; tel: 918.663.7060; fax: 918.663.7058; toll-free: 866.367.6232.

Here are five ways you can find a career counselor in your area.

1. Most states have counselor licensure laws and state boards that oversee this licensing process. Check your local phone directory under state government or check with your public library for the address and phone number of your state counselor licensing board. You may contact them for a list of licensed counselors or to check the credentials of a specific counselor.

2. Online, look for categories such as "career counseling," "vocational counseling," or "employment counseling." As you scan the names, check to see if the professionals describe their credentials. When you call, ask questions such as the following:

   - Are you a Fellow of the NCDA, a Master Career Counselor, or a Master Career Development Professional? (In California, ask if he or she is a Registered Professional Career Counselor.)

   - Are you licensed to practice counseling or psychology in this state?

   - Are you a member of a national or state career counseling professional association?

- What special training or prior certification do you have in the area of career counseling?

- Do you offer a free first session to evaluate the possibility of a good fit.

3. Ask colleagues, friends, and family members for the names of helpful career counselors with whom they have worked.

4. Check with the library to find lists of career services available through educational and community agencies such as community colleges, public school adult education programs, state employment services, vocational rehabilitation, or special career services. Websites such as www.careercounselorsne.org or www.careercc.org/ will also provide valuable information.

5. Life coaching is another category of help that offers similar services to career counseling (check out www.thecoachingdirectory.com for more information).

Go explore

Exploration will be an important aspect of your life for the next few years as you make important decisions about your future. Understand that your awareness of life possibilities is limited and anything you can do to broaden your knowledge will help you discover opportunities. In your planning, keep a running list of resources that you find throughout the year, and make sure to set aside time each week for research.

REMEMBER

❖ You need your own resource community that can help you find important information about your life dream and direction.

❖ Your desires and vision will feel fragile at first and they need some protection.

❖ You do not need to find something to do that no one else is doing. If there is a need in the world, there will likely be many people pursuing a similar dream.

❖ Swing within yourself. Don't shrink back, but also don't charge forward. Find a rhythm that is smooth, deliberate, focused, persistent, and calm.

❖ When we feel overwhelmed, confused, fearful or lost, we need to hear someone say: "You're not strange, sometimes life is just difficult."

CHAPTER SIX

TAKE YOUR CHANCES

A great hitter in baseball will fail seven out of ten times. If you only fail six out of ten times you will be inducted into the hall of fame.

"Security is mostly a superstition. It does not exist in nature, nor do the children of men as a whole experience it. Avoiding danger is no safer in the long run than outright exposure. Life is either a daring adventure or nothing."

— *Helen Keller*

Years ago when I was visiting my parents in Las Vegas, NV, I borrowed their car to run an errand. Upon returning, I pulled into the driveway and walked into the house. I was initially surprised that my parents, at their age, were able to redecorate and replace all their furniture in the short amount of time I was gone. And when I turned to them on the couch to ask them what happened to all their furniture, I noticed that these people were not my parents. My brain was having a difficult time processing what was happening. It only lasted a few seconds but everything felt like it was moving in slow motion. About to ask these strange people why they were in my parent's house and what they did with them, one of these strangers smiled at me and simply asked, "Wrong house?"

My parents live in one of these neighborhoods where all the houses look similar and in my haste, I'd pulled into a driveway two doors down. By the casual way this nice man asked me the question, I'm assuming it happens often.

The fact is, sometimes we get it wrong. We're not perfect and we make mistakes. Sadly, we have learned that mistakes are signs that we're either not trying hard enough or we are less than we ought to be. Standing there in the house of these neighbors, all I could do was smile back, say "oh, sorry," and walk out. It would be nice if I could handle all my mistakes so quickly and calmly.

Dealing with feelings of risk and the possibility of failure are important topics for discussion when seeking to discover and live your dreams. Everyone has a different level of tolerance for the uncomfortable feelings of risk and failure. There will always be a balance between our need for security and the reality of risk. No one could survive a life that is all risk and no safety, but we must become comfortable with the feelings associated with risk if we hope to move toward the life we want.

> *"The dangers of life are infinite, and among them is safety."*
>
> — *Goethe*

Risk Aversion

Aversion to risk is often the reason we get stuck. But we seldom realize this is what is going on. We call it by other names, like "being smart" or "realistic" or "practical." But everyone who has ever achieved their dream life did so by occasionally acting in ways that could be called foolish, unlikely, or unreasonable. Risky is sometimes the way it feels when you are pursuing your dream. You are taking chances and that means those chances won't always work out exactly as expected. But if we can understand why risk is important, the anxiety associated with it will lessen.

So let's begin by asking why risk feels so–risky. We are paralyzed by risk because we do not like to fail. The experience of failure is too often viewed as a commentary on our capabilities or value, rather than simply the way we learn. Renegotiate your relationship with failure and you will be better equipped to embrace risk. To do this, you will have to overcome the messages in your head that equate failure with shame.

Carl Yung called shame the "soul eating emotion." He talked about failing drawing class when he was in school. He says, "But my fear of failure and my sense of smallness in face of the vast world around me created in me not only a dislike but a kind of silent despair which completely ruined school for me. In addition, I was exempted from drawing classes on grounds of utter incapacity."[1] When a failure tells us we *are* a mistake rather than we *made* a mistake, we are feeling shame. Shame tells us we are defective and our mistakes are the proof. Shame is the emotion that prevents us from learning and we are all prone to it.

Just today, I had a minor example of shame in action. I was returning from lunch for my next appointment and had a cup of water in my hands. I was carrying a few other things and reached into my pocket for my keys when I accidently let the cup of water slip out of my hands and spill over the front of my pants. Without thinking I said, "Stupid idiot."

Really? Stupid idiot? For accidently spilling water on myself? Why? Am I so conditioned to shame that I punish myself for accidents? We do that kind of thing without even thinking, don't we? Why do we believe that we should never make a mistake?

Since kindergarten we have been taught to follow instructions and play by the rules. Innovation or initiative was usually not encouraged except in narrow settings or under certain controlled conditions. We were rarely, if ever, rewarded for our ability to think outside the box or to practice taking chances. Why did our errors on tests always get marked with big red X's? I grew up hating the color red. Maybe mistakes should get marked by green smiley faces that communicate, "Yippy, another chance to learn."

In the 8th grade, when first learning algebraic formulas, I thought I had come up with a quicker way to solve a problem. I thought it would be fun to come up with my own formula. I put the answer on a test and showed the creative process I used to come up with the solution. All of you know immediately how this story ends. It isn't even a surprise to learn that I wasn't at all rewarded for my effort to find a quicker and more efficient way to get the answer. What I got was an X next to my work, and a C on the test. I didn't get the answer in the correct way, and that was all there was to it.

But was that really "all there was to it?" Being correct is essential, particularly in math, and later I understood why that specific process was important, but it isn't the only thing we need an ability to do in life. Where do we practice innovation and creativity? What we do every day becomes the life we live, whether we want that life or not.

Do you want a life where you always get the right answer, or a life where you seek better ways to solve problems, do a job or reach your dream? I'm guessing that the 9th century mathematician Al-Khwarizmi, who is credited with discovering algebra, did so after many attempts and failures and probably amid much criticism. We need more than the ability to parrot Al-Khwarizmi's solutions. We also need to develop the ability to imitate his creative process and his courage.

Trained to Follow Directions
In John Taylor Gatto's book, *Weapons of Mass Instruction*, he makes some important observations about the limitations of public education. Gatto was a public educator in Manhattan for thirty years and retired the year after he was awarded Teacher of the Year by the state of New York. He makes this comment about risk:

> *We could encourage the best qualities of youthfulness—curiosity, adventure, resilience, the capacity for surprising insight—simply by being more flexible about time, texts, and tests, by introducing kids to truly competent adults, and by giving each student the autonomy he or she needs in order to take a risk every now and then.[2]*

But the real crime, as Gatto so boldly details, is the effort of the school system to create adults who know how to follow directions, do what they're told, not complain, not be unique, and to be on time. He says that public education was originally designed to help young people prepare for employment in the growing American industrial complex where competent workers needed the above abilities. Many of these skills are still useful and important, however, the world and its needs have changed, and these abilities are no longer enough. What is missing are the opportunities to learn and practice being creative, brave, unique, resourceful, and resilient in order to meet the demands of a changing society.

As we begin to understand what is necessary to fulfill our own dreams and interests, we must take responsibility for our own learning and especially for those areas left out by our formal education. Renegotiating our relationship with failure and practicing the skills associated with taking risks, we can begin to reach forward with courage.

I am amazed by how many graduates have been learning how to take risks in spite of an educational process that doesn't reward such efforts. You may have had a teacher or two who helped you reach outside the box and think imaginatively and creatively, but these opportunities are too infrequent to counter a mentality that encourages an avoidance of failure and an aversion to risk.

As an emerging adult, you are braving this unknown territory out of necessity. Safer roads are no longer available, so you must experiment with taking risks even though you are unprepared for the feelings of uncertainty and instability that come with it.

Risk Management
All successful people talk about their many failures on their road to success.

Before Walt Disney built his empire, he was fired by a newspaper editor because "he lacked imagination and had no good ideas." When Walt first tried to get MGM studios to distribute Mickey Mouse in 1927, he was told that the idea would never work because a giant mouse on the screen would terrify women.

Before J.K. Rowling had any "Harry Potter" success, the writer was a divorced single mother struggling on welfare while also attending school and writing a novel. Harry Potter was initially rejected by over a dozen publishers.

At age of 22, Oprah Winfrey was fired from her job as a television reporter because she was told she was "unfit for TV."

Before landing "I Love Lucy," Lucille Ball was widely regarded as a failed actress and a B-movie star and even dubbed "Queen of the B's" in the 1940s.

In his first screen test, the testing director of MGM noted that Fred Astaire, "Can't act. Can't sing. Slightly bald. Can dance a little."

After his first audition, Sidney Poitier, who grew up poor in the Bahamas, was told by the casting director, "Why don't you stop wasting people's time and go out and become a dishwasher or something?"

Three-time Oscar-winning filmmaker Oliver Stone dropped out of Yale to write his first novel, which was later rejected by publishers. When it was finally published in 1998, the novel was not well-received and Stone moved to Vietnam to teach English.

Steven Spielberg was rejected from the University of Southern California School of Theater, Film and Television three times.

When The Beatles were just starting out, a recording company told them, "No." Decca Recording studios said, "We don't like their sound, and guitar music is on the way out. They have no future in show business."

In 1973, Stephen King was working as an English teacher in Maine and selling short stories on the side to make ends meet. He received over 20 rejections for his first novel, "Carrie." One publisher wrote, "We are not interested in science fiction which deals with negative utopias. It will never sell."

After being cut from his high school basketball team, a young Michael Jordan went home and cried in the privacy of his bedroom.

Steve Jobs was a college dropout, a fired tech executive and an unsuccessful businessman. At 30-years-old he was devastated after being removed from the company he founded. In a 2005 commencement speech at Stanford University, Jobs explained,

> I didn't see it then, but it turned out that getting fired from Apple was the best thing that could have ever happened to me. The heaviness of being successful was replaced by the lightness of being a beginner again, less sure about everything. It freed me to enter one of the most creative periods of my life.[3]

Before he was Wolverine on "X-Men" or a Broadway star, actor Hugh Jackman got fired from his cashier job at 7-Eleven because he talked too much to the customers.

In 1954, Elvis was still a no-name performer, and Jimmy Denny, manager of the Grand Ole Opry, fired him after just one performance saying, "You ain't goin' nowhere, son. You ought to go back to drivin' a truck."

There are thousands of these stories and they make us feel hopeful for a time, but we may still walk away feeling frozen or unmotivated about our own dream and pessimistic about achieving the life we want. We are afraid to fail and paralyzed by risk.

You may feel far away from your dreams and aspirations and may even wonder if focusing on them is a waste of time. But realize that good planning and resourcing can help you deal with the risk and potential failure associated with doing the work.

> *"Progress always involves risk; you can't steal second base and keep your foot on first."*
> — *Frederick Wilcox*

Risk and Planning

For many years, Sue and I had an interest in remodeling houses. Sue had some training in interior design and I have always loved working with my hands; plus we liked the idea of working together. We had remodeled our own homes over the years and thought we'd like to try and buy a house, fix it up, and then sell it. We had this desire and dream long before HGTV was invented and when "flip" was still something you did off a diving board. But for years we never did anything about it. I think the riskiness of the idea stymied us. So about fifteen years ago, while doing some reading on planning and goal setting, we decided to break the dream down into some manageable pieces.

What exactly would it take for us to make this dream a reality? We came up with six or seven smaller steps that would get us to our ultimate goal. Some of the steps included: call real estate agents to learn about the community, contact builders to discuss materials and labor prices, talk to the bank about getting loans, contact a few other investors who did similar work, check out some books on remodeling, drive through neighbor-hoods to find prime locations, and spend several days looking at homes for sale. Even developing these small steps felt risky because the overall objective was so intimidating.

In order to manage the risk, we had to consciously set aside thoughts of the overall goal and just concentrate on the smaller parts. We told ourselves that we could pull the plug on the whole thing at any time. As we moved forward in the process, step by step, the risk was managed and the fear of failure did not im-mobilize us. When it finally came time for us to purchase our first piece of property, we were still nervous, but we were prepared. We had gained much more knowledge and understanding about the business and dealt with the feelings of risk all along the way.

If safety was our only value, and risk the primary foe, then we would never have considered this path in the first place. Dreams and desires are kept safely tucked away behind good excuses and reasonable thinking. Now that we have bought and sold many houses we are far more comfortable with the feelings of risk associated with doing something we want to do and that brings us great satisfaction and fulfillment. We have learned from our many mistakes but we had the confidence to make important adjustments, and keep moving forward.

You do not need to be prepared for a risk you are not ready to take. One of the reasons to break up the dream into daily and weekly tasks is because it also breaks up the risky feelings into smaller, more manageable pieces. This is because any failure associated with the smaller task is not a failure of the overall goal. Consequently the feeling of risk is less intense.

Those who achieve success do so by working hard and cre-atively in the face of risk and failure. Edison and others like him who attempted lofty projects and dreams needed to stay focused on the daily experiment or task in order to avoid feeling overwhelmed by the risk of the larger objective.

> *"I have not failed. I've just found 10,000 ways that don't work."*
> — *Thomas Edison in discussing the invention of the light bulb.*

If the next task is one that is unfamiliar and difficult to figure out, don't get ahead of yourself. Focus your energy on the job in front of you rather than the one around the next bend. No one can guarantee what will become of your efforts, but doing your work for today is the only way you will find out, and something good happens when you are willing to press ahead and risk failure on the daily task.

Failure and Success
Experiences of failure are an important part of every success and indicate that we are taking significant risks. If we never fail, we may not be risking enough. Failure will be a part of every process that moves you toward your unique dreams and aspirations, so don't be surprised or sidetracked by it.

So fearing failure is how it will feel when you are attempting something you want, but can hardly imagine having. We will talk more about fear in a later chapter, but for now pay attention to taking risks in the areas connected to your dreams and passions.

The only failure you need to worry about is the failure of not taking your dream seriously enough to decide what daily or weekly steps you will take to make it a reality. When Sue and I started the step by step process of our housing effort, we had little confidence that the dream of buying a house, fixing it up and selling it would actually happen. But the only real failure for us at that time would have been to not carefully plan the necessary steps. Not taking that planning step would guarantee that our goals and desires would never happen.

Here is the silver lining in the daily cloud of risk: When you succeed with the smaller task, you end up feeling more hopeful about the overall goal. This is why it continues to be important to break up your dream into smaller and smaller segments and to schedule a day and time when each task will be accomplished.

If someone dreams of becoming a diamond cutter and one of the steps for the month is to visit a nearby jewelry store, it won't be enough to have it on your to-do list. Proper planning requires you to choose the store, determine the day, and settle on a particular time to go. Until you have that specific day and time written down, as well as a measurable objective, your goal will not feel reachable, and the feelings of risk might deflate you.

Debilitating and paralyzing feelings of risk may signify that your plans are not specific enough. And you can assume this is the case if weeks go by without taking any action toward living your dream. Without a plan, our dreams stay only in our head and we have little chance of living them.

Risk and Hope

The decision to follow your heart will become a way to live the rest of your life with hope, because at this stage of the game, the future remains uncertain. No one knows what might happen. So why not live your life in a way that gives your loftiest dreams a chance? Even if your hopes don't come true exactly as you imagine, you will have developed a skill; the skill of taking deliberate and focused chances, which will become an important part of everything you do.

Instead of settling for the obviously attainable, learn how to reach out, stretch forward, and work daily for the life you want to live. Why not? What do you have to lose? Decide to become someone who is always working toward your dream, seeking to accomplish your heart's desire, and fighting for something you really want to do. This is an important aspect of living your life with hope.

> I think the biggest thing for me was to get out of my head and just try things! Without risk and the possibility of making mistakes, it's hard to really know what path is right for you. I've been so pleasantly surprised by new interests and passions I've discovered.
>
> Tammy, 2007

In John Maxwell's book, *"Failing Forward,"* he discusses our relationship to failure and describes it as one of the most important parts the success process. "If you can change the way you see failure, you can gain the strength it takes to keep running the race. Get a new definition of failure. Regard it as the price you pay for progress."[4]

Failure is what you will experience over and over again if you are moving toward your dream. If you never fail, then you may be playing it way too safe. Failure is how we learn. You would have never learned to walk if you hadn't been willing to fall. In fact, just putting your dreams on paper might feel too scary, intimidating, or even stupid. But this is where the battle begins, right here in the simple things, in the first steps.

Listen to Julien Smith in his book *The Flinch* talk about failure: "Kids naturally begin this way. It's why their world is always growing. They find hurdles, jump them, and get stronger. When they see they made it, they move on to bigger hurdles. If they fall down, they try again later. It's a basic cycle. It's how kids figure out they can eventually change the world . . . It's a process."[5]

But as we get older and the challenges get harder, we experience more pain from falling down. Consequently, the anticipation of pain is the basis of the flinch. We can easily forget that the only way forward involves struggling against the instinct to avoid pain.

In all sports, the ability to handle failure plays a huge part in becoming successful. Because failure is often attached to shame, it naturally becomes something to avoid at all costs. It is a common belief that, whenever possible, one should avoid situations where the chance of failure exists. It feels safer and wiser to move toward sure things. But consider this: a great hitter in baseball will fail *seven* out of ten times. If they fail *six* out of ten times they make it into the Baseball Hall of Fame.

Rejection Therapy

For many years, entrepreneurship training programs would ask students to become door to door sales people for a couple of months. Dozens of doors slammed in your face every day was viewed as a great way to overcome the fear of rejection as well as take the debilitating sting out of failure.

Robert D. Smith in his book, *20,000 Days and Counting*, writes about his years as a door-to-door book salesman:

> *Rejection is a part of life that we have been trained to find unpleasant. But what if every rejection only meant you were one step closer to a yes? What if you considered rejection to be a crucial part of your search instead of an obstacle? What if it were merely a chapter in the much larger story of your purpose?*[6]

So Smith took a different approach. He decided that getting no's would become his new objective; every day he would try and get 30 no's from his door-to-door efforts. That way, even if he didn't sell anything, he would still accomplish his goal. He says that he rarely received 30 no's before he received at least one yes which led him to recognize the no's as simply part of the success process.[7]

Jia Jang is a blogger who wanted to be an entrepreneur and knew that all entrepreneurs needed the ability to face rejection and manage failure. In an effort to improve his ability to do this, he decided to orchestrate one rejection per day for a hundred days.[8] He called it "Rejection Therapy" after a game invented by Jason Comely.[9]

Some of his tasks were: Ask a stranger to borrow 100 dollars, request a "burger refill" from a fast food restaurant, ask a donut shop to make an Olympic symbol donut for him, ask to deliver a pizza for Dominos, become a live mannequin at Abercrombie, give a weather report on live TV, and sit in the driver's seat of a police car. Although he did occasionally get a yes, for the most part, his requests resulted in the-hoped-for rejection.

When questioned in interviews about his tactic for handling rejection, Jang says that the technique is simply about the practice. As he grew more accustomed and familiar with the feelings of rejection, he became much better at dealing with it, and more importantly, less resistant toward actions that might result in it.

Failure is a teacher that gives us the opportunity to learn and adjust. Half-way through Jia's rejection therapy process, he noticed that he was getting a few more yes's to his requests than at the beginning. He says, "I have learned more about communication and human connection in the past month than I had in my two years of business school. I have learned how to make a crazy request, stay calm and negotiate."[10]

Failure doesn't mean you're not good enough, it just means you're trying something that is difficult and challenging. One of Jia's daily challenges was to ask a TV station if he could do the weather. So later that month, while being interviewed on a morning news program, he asked his interviewer if he could give the weather report that morning.

He received the anticipated rejection but later he writes:

> With lights and camera in my face, the pressure was on. It would be tough to pursue my request after the first no, like I did in other situations. However, this was two days in a row when I didn't ask 'why' after the initial rejection, which I'm not proud of. Also, I should have offered alternatives, such as asking her to talk to the producer, and maybe invite me back after my 100 days for the weather forecast.[11]

Of course, rejection and failure are not the goals in life. Nobody wants to simply be good at handling rejection. The objective, however, is to become less afraid of trying things that might end in rejection or failure. We can discover that failure is not the debilitating, shaming and humiliating experience we've always feared. Most people who achieve their dreams are people who were able to renegotiate their relationship to risk and failure, and become less and less resistant to confronting them.

Give your own rejection therapy a try. It is definitely a lot more difficult than you might imagine. You will confront your instinct to avoid embarrassment but you will also notice that each day that impulse will lessen in intensity. Start out simple, but be sure your requests are extreme enough to get rejected.

Rejection Therapy

Make a list of fourteen challenges that will result in a rejection. Do nothing unsafe or illegal but something that will cause you to receive a "no" answer. Do one of these activities each day for fourteen days.

Examples:

Day 1 – Call your cell phone company and ask them if they could give you one free month of service for graduating from college.

Day 2 – Ask the manager at your grocery store if he'd let you sample the different types of milk in the store to see which one you like best.

Day 3 – Ask a police officer if he would take your picture wearing his badge or wearing his handcuffs to send to your mom.

Day 4 – Ask someone to borrow twenty dollars.

In baseball, occasionally one of the players would develop a fear of getting hit with the ball. The slight, almost unnoticeable flinch just as a pitcher released the ball had a tremendous effect on a batter's ability to hit successfully. The way our coaches occasionally dealt with this problem was to put the player in the batter's box and throw tennis balls at him for several minutes each day from about twenty-feet away. The hitter would get used to balls flying at him and slowly begin to lose his fear of getting hit. It is true that a tennis ball doesn't hurt as much as a hard ball, but it remedied the fearful anticipation, which in turn, corrected the flinch. Now would be a good time to begin a list of activities you may be avoiding in your life simply because you are afraid you might fail.

Embrace Risk

Failure or rejection is not a sign that something is wrong with you, but rather are opportunities to learn more about your approach or your direction. Begin now and take your chances in reaching toward your dream. Go back to one of the dreams you described in Chapter Three and review the steps you outlined for achieving it. Ask the question, "Have I excluded any steps simply because they feel too risky?"

When we were planning our remodeling business, I had outlined the steps necessary for achieving this dream, but later I realized that I subconsciously omitted, *"submit offers on possible houses."* I am fairly certain I did this because putting an offer in on a house was such a frightening step that I avoided even writing it down. I later learned that there is always a seven to ten day inspection period during which time an offer can be rescinded. Since then we have put in dozens of offers on houses that didn't work out because, either we weren't the highest bidder or, after further inspection, the house would be too costly to rehab. In your planning, don't be afraid to include steps you can't imagine yourself doing at the moment. You may learn things later that will make the step feel much more achievable.

You want to take risks that lead you to your goals, but aren't so big that the game is over if you fail. In the housing business, we needed to be willing to fail, but we always wanted to be sure that any failure did not put an end to our business. It took us longer to find the right deals, but we wanted to be sure that we could always get our original money out even if we didn't make a profit. That way we could learn from our mistakes and make improvements on the next one.

ASKING FOR A JOB

In this exercise you will practice asking for a job and getting rejected.

Go to your downtown area or to a mall. Start at one end of the mall and go into EVERY store and ask to speak with the manager. Tell the manager you are looking for a job and want to know if they have any openings. Tell him/her that you are willing to do anything. After each one, write down the basic results of the conversation. Do not skip any store no matter what it is. You do not need to take the job. If they say yes, get an application. Do this exercise for one hour.

Store name	Manager's name	Response	Follow up

Risk is hard. Recently, I made an offer to a group of students that I would give any one of them a hundred dollars to begin a small business during the current semester. All they needed to do was present a basic business plan that made sense and I would fund their effort. They would need to substantiate their work, show receipts, and then follow through on their plan. At the end of the three month period they would repay the loan and keep whatever profits they made. I told them I would help them with anything they might need along the way except I would not provide the business idea. And if the business didn't work, they would not need to repay the loan.

I was surprised that not one student took me up on the offer. Either no one had the confidence that they could make a profit, or they were unwilling to risk failure even with someone else's money. My sense is they did not see the important connection between this exercise and their future.

We are taught to desire success, but we are not taught to be unafraid of failure. So why not try this exercise for yourself. Take a hundred dollars and try to turn it into a hundred-fifty dollars in three months. Begin by making a list of possible businesses you can start in order to make a profit. Give it a try for three months. Look online for short term money making ideas and design a business plan. Execute the plan and respond to difficulties and problems along the way. Take a risk. You will learn many things from the experiment.

REMEMBER

❖ The experience of failure is too often viewed as a commentary on our capabilities or value, rather than the way we learn.

❖ You want to take risks that lead you to your goals but aren't so big that the game is over if you fail.

❖ Even if your hopes don't come true exactly as you imagine, you have developed the skill of taking deliberate and focused chances, which becomes an important part of everything you do.

❖ Don't forget that the way forward involves the struggle against the instinct to avoid pain.

❖ We are taught to desire success, but we are not taught to be unafraid of failure.

❖ Mistakes and failures will be a part of every endeavor and every process that moves you toward your dreams, so don't be surprised or sidetracked by them.

SUMMER
PROTECTION AND ENDURANCE

In many parts of the world, summer can be as challenging as winter. It is still the growing season but the heat and occasional dryness can create stress and strain on plants and animals. Even humans can struggle with survival in the extremely hot temperatures of summer. It is possible that more vegetation may be lost during the heat of summer than even the cold of winter. Plants will often seal off their pores during the driest months and use their reserves of water and carbohydrates to survive, synthesizing more proteins during the night when it is cooler. Sunlight is important for all living things; but the dry, hot, long summer can also bring challenges and difficulties to even the most robust ecosystem.

It is hard to keep going during the summer months. It is easy to lose steam or get discouraged. This is definitely true when discussing the challenge of working toward the life you desire because it is not a quick journey. We must be braced for a much longer trip. In the next four chapters we will talk about some of the many difficulties that can sideline our efforts or interrupt our progress.

In Chapter Seven, we talk about discouragement, which can assault us anytime we take on a difficult task. Even those projects that generate tremendous enthusiasm at the start, can hit the rough roads of discouragement before the end is even in view.

In Chapter Eight, we discuss how to handle solitude in a positive and constructive way. After college, many of our projects and endeavors will happen in isolation. In school we were always surrounded by an abundance of other people who were on a similar path, but not so much anymore.

A third challenge to our endurance is fear. Nothing can interrupt our progress as quickly as our tendency to shrink back from difficulty because we are afraid. Fear is a disease that can attack us during the weakened state of the summer slump. In Chapter Nine, we will talk about how to deal with this potential menace to our advancement and growth.

The final chapter in this section describes a skill that is vital if we hope to survive the blistering onslaught of summer drought. Gratitude operates like a refreshing summer rain, showing up just in time, clearing out the humidity, chasing away menacing bugs and providing a moment of renewal, clarity and hope.

In order to get to the harvest, we must survive the summer. The skills described in the next few chapters will help us stay strong and keep moving forward in the face of threatening difficulties.

CHAPTER SEVEN

BATTLE DISCOURAGEMENT

Imagine a large enemy force gathered before you, ready to block your advance and kill your dreams. This is what you are up against. Living the life you desire will be won or lost on these daily, or sometimes hourly, battlefields.

"In spite of everything I shall rise again: I will take up my pencil, which I have forsaken in my great discouragement, and I will go on with my drawing."
— *Vincent Van Gogh*

After graduating from New York University Medical School, Jonas Salk was invited to spend a year in the research laboratory with his professor of biochemistry Dr. Thomas Francis. This meant leaving his class and adding an additional year to his program. Later he saw this as one of the most important decisions of his life. As Salk said, "I believe that this is all linked to my original ambition or desire, which was to be of some help to humankind in the field of medicine." At the end of his residency, Salk applied for a permanent research position, but many of the positions had Jewish quotas so were closed to him. Dr. Francis found extra grant money to have Salk work with him as they developed a flu vaccine for the army.

Since first identified in 1789, polio baffled doctors and terrified parents. In 1914 and 1919 there were terrible polio epidemics in the United States. In 1952, 58,000 cases were reported. Polio was the most frightening public health problem in the postwar world. The outbreaks appeared random and children were most affected. Polio affects the brain and spinal cord and often results in paralysis or death from respiratory problems. Parents watched helplessly as their otherwise healthy children were struck with this terrible virus.

Salk was asked to join the research team to help find a cure. He was integral to the process, not only as a researcher, but also a motivator. Personally however, Salk often felt discouraged. According to Leon Gutterman, "Progress in his research was slow and occasionally he felt frustrated. He even thought about giving up his virus research completely. But one day, when this urge was particularly strong, he was sitting in a park watching children play and he remembered again why he was doing it. There were thousands of children and adults who would never walk again and whose bodies would be paralyzed because of polio. He realized his awesome responsibility and so he continued his task with renewed vigor."[1]

Salk spent sixteen hours per day, seven days a week in the lab which he later described as "two and a half years of drudgery and hard work." One elderly associate observed, "That boy really suffers when he sees a paralytic case. You look at him and you see him thinking, 'My God, this can be prevented.'"[2]

In 1954, after hundreds of hours of research and experiments, Dr. Salk, his wife and three sons were given the vaccine. "He felt that he couldn't ask other parents to let him give this vaccine to their children if he wasn't willing to first try it on his own."[3] In 1955 the announcement was made by the University of Michigan, "the vaccine was safe and effective." Europeans listened over the Voice of America, church bells rang, moments of silence were observed, parents and teachers wept, and spontaneous celebrations erupted. Jonas Salk had changed the world.

When Quitting Feels Good

Evan, a recent graduate, called me to discuss his desire to do some humanitarian work overseas. He had been thinking about various possibilities for his life and thought it would be interesting to live in another country and do something meaningful. Since leaving college, he had been living at home and sending out résumés in an effort to find a full time job. For the past several months he worked part-time as a dog groomer, a job he had while in high school. He sounded discouraged, so I asked him if overseas humanitarian work was what he really wanted to do with his life, or just something to pass the time.

He was quiet for a minute and then admitted honestly that he was discouraged and wanted a break from feeling so hopeless. When I asked him about his interests, he said that he had wanted to make films, but his beginning attempts didn't work out very well. Someone told him that to work in the film industry he would need to live in either New York or Los Angeles, and this didn't interest him. When I asked him what he had done next, he simply said, "Not much."

The impulse to quit and just "take life as it comes" will be a difficult temptation to resist throughout the dreaming/planning process. You will want to push off these issues until later in your life, feeling like you are still young and have all the time in the world to "get serious" and plan. But you need to be careful. You are young, but the skills, and more importantly, the habits you are forming now will become the foundation of the way you function in the future.

This could be the most important chapter so far, because it is about the temptation to quit the process even before you actually begin the work. It is the only real thing that threatens your chances of discovering and living your dream life. You may think that the temptation to quit is simply a small nuisance that can be overcome with a little extra effort. You may be tempted to believe that there are many other skills more important to living your dream than simply sticking with it—but you'd be mistaken.

> When I graduated from college I was filled with enthusiasm. I had a lot of ideas and energy. I'm surprised that I became disheartened so quickly. I think I felt overwhelmed by not knowing exactly what I was supposed to do.
>
> Jennifer, 2007

Here is all you really need to know about quitting: ready? Whatever causes you to stop working on the life you really want, whatever name you give it, is the impulse to quit and give up. And the better the excuse sounds, the more powerful the impulse.

I'm too young.
I'm not good enough.
I'm not smart enough.
I'm too tired.
I have no place to think.

I'll do it next month.
My feet hurt.
I need a break.
I'm not making any progress.
This is dumb.
Who do I think I'm kidding?
None of my friends are doing this.
I just want to relax.
I'm confused.
I don't know who I am.
I need to just focus on the here and now.
I can't think about someday.
I just want to be happy.
I only want to have fun.
I don't care about my dream.

Each one of these thoughts, no matter how true, is simply an effort to get you to stop trying. When we let these ideas begin to seep into our brains, they trigger the emotional response of discouragement. And discouragement is the precursor to quitting. Quitting feels good for a moment because it relieves the pressure of discouragement.

> *"The most important thing about art is to work. Nothing else matters except sitting down every day and trying."*
>
> — *Steven Pressfield*

Your Lizard Brain

Any thought or attitude that disrupts your enthusiasm, your drive, or your motivation is nothing more than an attempt by your resistance to keep you safe and out of harm's way. Seth Godin calls this your "lizard brain." He uses the term *lizard* because he sees this as an older evolutionary part of our humanity, whose main objective was to protect us from predators and guard us from unsafe situations.[4]

You may wonder what is so harmful or dangerous about seeking your dream and working toward the life you want? Just this; when we reach out for what we really want, we risk failure, embarrassment and humiliation, which feels extremely dangerous. Every instinct that would lead you to quit or lose steam is your lizard brain telling you to stop being foolish and just survive the day. In these moments, when your enthusiasm is at its lowest and you feel unmotivated and even angry, one of your biggest mistakes will be to not see this as an attack on your dreams.

Imagine a large enemy force gathered before you, with the latest weaponry and the most skilled warriors, ready to block your advance and kill your dreams for good. This is what you are up against. Living the life you desire will be won or lost on these daily, or sometimes hourly, battlefields.

Let's assume you have lost your motivation and enthusiasm, and now your dreams feel less possible, more distant, and frankly, not achievable. Here is what you must do; continue to work your plan. This is precisely why you have a plan. If you were always motivated, excited, energized, and inspired, having a plan wouldn't be nearly as important. But the

When I was in college I was very good at handling pressure and stressful situations. My class assignments would pile up but I knew what I needed to do to survive. Now, as a graduate, I'm less capable at handling the stress. I think it's because I'm not sure what I should be doing.

Travis, 2006

existence of a plan is to help deal with your lizard brain when it takes over and tells you to give up.

When Evan's lizard brain told him that working on films was a stupid and unrealistic dream, he quit. And discouragement won because he didn't have a plan to fall back on for defense. Your best weapon in the face of unrelenting discouragement and the impulse to quit is your clear, daily plan. You will discover that as you do your work in spite of these assaults, your feelings will change and you'll get over the hump. If this is not possible, and your discouragement has you paralyzed, then you will need to do some "remedial imagining."

Begin Again
Go back to the work of Chapter Three and read again about your dream. Enter into the fantasy of the life you want to live. Do not rely on your memory at this point. You must read the words you wrote throughout this journey and begin again to remember the future as you imagined it.

Re-Imagining

Pretend you are describing your dream to your best friend for the first time. Write it out again using new words and images. Describe in detail why you are interested in this endeavor. What makes it so attractive and exciting?

_____

_____

_____

_____

Those feelings are still there and it is simply your resistance clouding your energy and motivation. Do not underestimate its power. You will not want to go back and review. The opposition in your brain will tell you it will not do any good. It will tell you that it won't work and that it was foolish to think you could do what you wanted. You will need a conscious, courageous and stubborn decision to believe and fight on.

> *"Every great work, every big accomplishment, has been brought into manifestation through holding to the vision, and often just before the big achievement, comes apparent failure and discouragement."*
> — *Florence Scovel Shinn*

Sometimes we get discouraged because we lose patience. You are developing a collection of skills that are meant to carry you throughout your life, not just the next few years. Putting pressure on yourself or expecting too much, too soon, will only make the journey more stressful and disheartening. This is a marathon run, not a sprint. So relax, breathe, and continue to move forward, one day at a time.

Discouragement is not just a possibility. It is a guarantee. You will want to quit. If you made it to this chapter then you do have enough resolve to survive these difficult periods, but don't be naively tricked into thinking it won't happen to you, or that it will be easy to overcome.

Take Action

Every endeavor I have ever pursued has been riddled with periods of extreme discouragement and the instinct to quit. Several years ago, I was tasked with finishing my dissertation for my doctoral degree and I was down to my final four months. This University required that my degree be completed in eight years from matriculation to graduation and I had been in the program seven years, eight months and four days. I finished all the course work in three years and had procrastinated on finishing the dissertation for an additional four. I had applied for an extension to the program each year and was down to my final few months. In a conversation with my advisor I asked if another extension was possible and she simply said, "No Bob, you've run out of time."

She needed a finished product in four months. I didn't want to quit but my lizard brain was winning. I needed to remember the feelings I had when I first started the doctoral program, and my reasons for wanting this degree in the first place. So I worked out a plan with her and committed myself to submitting the rough draft in three months by writing four pages a day, five days a week. Two days a week I would do research and five days I would write. I wrote every morning from six until noon. I still had a job but arranged to cut back on my hours in order to finish the project.

I tell you this story for this reason; I wanted to give up and quit every morning; not just some mornings, every morning. It would start even before getting out of bed. In the dark I'd begin a mental list of all the reasons why I was not capable of finishing the task, and then I'd begin a mental list of all the other things I could be doing with my time. Then I would move to the fact that the topic was stupid and I wouldn't pass the examination. Then I'd spend a few minutes berating the University for its inflexible rules. As I lifted myself out of bed my lizard brain would finally begin to lose steam and I'd start to write. But the only reason I'd do so was because of the daily plan I had devised, nothing else. Write four pages every morning, five days a week was what got me through. Sometimes I'd feel extremely disheartened, but I'd sit there, feel the distress, and keep writing.

The result: Four months later, after several revisions, I turned in my final copy to my advisor, defended it, and there I was, receiving my doctoral degree a few months after that. The lizard brain is real, alive and well, and has been my traveling companion in the pursuit of all my life goals. I have never achieved anything without fighting the impulse to quit. If the project is important to you, then, at some point, you will want to give up.

Developing a clear picture of your dream life and working on a daily strategy is not the easiest way to live, particularly in the beginning. I have not, by any means, always lived with resolve, clarity and direction. But when those voices start up in your head, you will want to do whatever it takes to escape the uncomfortable thoughts and feelings brought on by your lizard brain. Quitting will be the quickest and easiest remedy for the pain. If you quit, especially with a fairly convincing reason, you will immediately feel better. Usually you will fill the empty space with lots of activities that can allow your mind to escape the discouragement. For a while you will feel relieved.

Uncertainty: The Lizard's Power

You must ask yourself a question before this happens to you, and you must write down the answer: Is living your dream and finding the life you desire more important than instant comfort? Most of you would probably say yes to that question. Your resistance therefore will begin the attack by casting tremendous doubt on the possibility of victory and then offer comfort in the place of the pain. It will tell you that success is a longshot anyway so why continue, why try?

If you believed that reaching your goals was a guarantee, discouragement and quitting would never stand a chance. Your lizard brain would slither off in certain defeat. Everyone would be willing to forgo some present comfort if they were assured success. But success is not a guarantee because the future is always uncertain.

But the skills you are learning in the dreaming and planning process will help you live the life you want, even if it is slightly different from the life you are now envisioning. Pursuing your dream is more than simply arriving at the anticipated destination. It takes you down a road that opens up new possibilities and opportunities that you would never have seen if you had given up and quit.

When you give up on the work because you do not think your dream is possible, you also quit on a process that has the power to change the world. Remember, you are learning more than just the pathway to a specific life. You are learning a pathway to any pusuit, at any of the various stages in your future.

When confronting your lizard brain, you are challenging certain instincts and habits that you've picked up through the years. Some of these will need to be unlearned and replaced. The idea that it was enough to sit still, pay attention, do what you're told, be on time, give the right answer, don't take risks, fear failure, and stand in line, will need careful re-evaluation. You are challenging many of these assumptions, and learning skills that will be as important as any particular dream you may have at this moment.

Despite only three years of formal education, Italian-born Rachele was a self-taught engineer and inventor. When he was only six years old, he asked his mother what made the water come up when she used the hand pump on the family well. She didn't know. He informed her that he would find out someday and tell her.

He had a natural curiosity and an industrious spirit. When he and his brother emigrated from Italy in the 1920's, they went into business together in Northern California, making props for airplanes and wind turbines for irrigating farms. They also produced pumps and filters for both wine and water. As the family grew so did their business. Their attitude of ingenuity, creativity and hard work became an important part of their family history.

But their most well-known invention came in 1943 after Kenneth, one of their many cousins, developed severe rheumatoid arthritis. The best treatment at the time was sitting in a metal tub of swirling water at a hospital. The family went to work to develop and manufacture a pump and air aspirator unit for a home tub, allowing the patient to relax and relieve pain without going to the hospital. The Jacuzzi family never set out to make therapeutic tubs or help people with arthritis. However, the industrial skills they had developed earlier allowed them to create a solution to ease the suffering of many, which they viewed as their most valuable and important accomplishment.[5]

> *"Have you ever heard someone say, an opportunity presented itself? I find that phrase misleading. As a rule, opportunities never "present themselves." Enterprising people discover them."*
> — *Remo Jacuzzi*

So when I tell you not to give up, I am saying more than don't give up on your dream. I am saying don't give up on learning the way all dreams are discovered and lived. When you get discouraged because your dream all of a sudden feels distant or impossible, try to remember that this isn't the most important part of this process. You are learning how to live with purpose and resolve. You are learning how to be intentional about what you want to do and how to formulate a specific plan to get there. You are learning and practicing a body of skills that will help you discover the life of your own choosing no matter what it is. And these skills will go with you through all the coming stages of your life.

Dealing with Fatigue

Occasionally, physical or emotional fatigue may be the source of your discouragement. Remember to listen to your body, and during moments of discouragement, make sure it isn't just an indication that you need to take a short break. Be careful that the "break" doesn't turn into procrastination, but fatigue can sometimes result in feeling low or disheartened. Therefore, consider the possibillity that you may need to take a couple days off.

Make a plan to do something fun or relaxing, especially if you have been working hard for a period of several weeks or months. Decide ahead of time when you will get back to your schedule. A good plan should already include times for relaxation and rest, but feelings of discouragement might mean you have been a little too aggressive in your strategy. Consider revisiting your approach in order to make sure you have enough space or variety in your life to avoid burn out.

Getting Re-energized

Name five activities that have the power to refuel your energy. Make a decision to do one of these this week.

1. _____

2. _____

3. _____

4. _____

5. _____

Reach Out to a Friend

During times of discouragement, especially when you feel stuck, you may need to get in touch with one of your trusted resources, someone who has been there as an encourager and fan from the beginning. It needs to be someone who won't simply give you advice, but will talk to you about your dream and give you needed affirmation.

It is in these times when you need to hear again, from someone you trust, that taking this risk, reaching forward for your dream, is one of the best decisions of your life. They need to reiterate to you what you already know but cannot feel in this moment. They need to remind you that you have nothing to lose but everything to gain by giving this a shot. Only if you quit, only if you give up, are your chances for success reduced to zero.

If you dream, if you plan, and if you continue to work your plan, you will succeed. You may not feel that assurance right now, but it doesn't make it untrue. You need to let that sink in. You need to know that the only thing standing between you and the life you want is your decision to not quit the process. As I said earlier, this is the best bad news you'll ever hear, but it's the truth.

Discouragement is hard. We've all faced it, more than once. It's difficult to ignore and it is hard to resist altering your plan because of it. Discouragement is that voice telling you that others may live their dream, but this option is not open to you. Then on the heels of discouragement is blame. You might blame your upbringing or you might blame your lack of talent or bad luck, but remember this is just the ploy of your resistance, trying to get you to quit.

If you resist discouragement's demand that you give up, discouragement will leave. It will surely return some other day in a slightly altered form, but the power of its voice will diminish for a time and allow you to continue your quest. Every morning during the writing of my dissertation, after the first few paragraphs, the resistance would subside for the moment. It would be back the next day, but as I worked my plan for the day, it would leave. This is why a clear and precise plan is so important. You will not always feel inspired to do your work, so having a specific daily plan is sometimes the only thing that allows you to keep going and not quit.

Evaluate the Dream–Renew the Plan
Your plans and dreams will remain fluid and open to change. There is more than one way to express your heart's desire or to make it a reality. One of the side benefits to discouragement is the opportunity to renew your vision. Every morning I needed to remind myself that this doctoral degree was truly something I wanted. You need to be extremely careful at this point. Do not alter your plan simply because you are discouraged, but use discouragement as motivation to revisit the details, the objective, and your approach.

It was Paul's dream to write and play music. He had a fairly clear vision about how that would look, and he worked hard to make it happen. But after a period of time, some of his expectations didn't pan out and he got discouraged. But instead of revisiting the plan and renegotiating his approach, he just kept banging away in a direction that clearly wasn't working until he became too tired to keep knocking.

Ryan was also a musician who faced similar hurdles and frustrations in his pursuits. His desire was to write musicals and perform on Broadway. It was a lofty goal that continues to guide his life plans to this day. However, the breaks didn't come right away so he adjusted his targets but kept moving toward them.

He is now teaching musical theater at a major university and continues to write and perform for the campus allowing hundreds to enjoy his creativity and talent. He has not forgotten or given up on his ultimate dream even though his strategy has been adjusted many times.

Keep working the plan you have chosen but don't be afraid to make changes and adjustments, when needed. Just to be clear, the discouragement is your invitation to look at the plan, not the authority to alter it. Alter the plan only because as you examine it, you decide that a new approach has more potential for success. Sometimes, if we don't panic, discouragement can produce new and creative breakthroughs.

Work the Plan – Win the Battle

To summarize, when discouragement raises its ugly head, the only thing that will get you back to your energy and enthusiasm is the decision to work your daily plan—nothing else. There is no special trick to this. It is basic and simple—but not easy. Discover your dream, make your plan, work the steps, and evaluate the results. Accept the fact that discouragement will occasionally be your traveling companion, but not one you want to trust for advice. You must simply continue to work your plan in the face of it—period.

REMEMBER

❖ The habits you are forming now will become the foundation of the way you function in the future.

❖ Your best weapon in the face of unrelenting discouragement and the impulse to quit is your clear, daily plan.

❖ When discouragement hits, remember again the future as you imagined it.

❖ It is not possible to achieve anything in life without fighting the impulse to quit.

❖ You are learning and practicing a body of skills that will help you discover the life of your own choosing no matter what it is.

❖ Do not alter your plan simply because you are discouraged, but use discouragement as motivation to revisit the details, the objective, and your approach.

CHAPTER EIGHT
PRACTICE SOLITUDE

Discovering your true desires and putting those hopes and dreams into a plan requires solitude. Time alone allows your mind to be at rest so it can speak to you.

"The best thinking has been done in solitude. The worst has been done in turmoil."
— *Thomas A. Edison*

"Without great solitude no serious work is possible."
— *Pablo Picasso*

For several years, I have invited recent college graduates to sit on a panel and describe some of the realities of post-college life. Current students listen with rapt attention to the challenges faced by these graduates as they now attempt to navigate their futures. Without fail, at some point in the conversation, those returning students will explain with pained clarity how difficult it is to discover meaningful friend-ships after college. One of the hardest adjustments to the post-graduate life is the shocking surprise of not being able to see your closest friends every day. You discover that you are alone much of the time and that takes some getting used to.

In college, anytime you wanted, you could drop by your friend's dorm room, go to the coffee shop, or visit the library, and im-mediately you'd be surrounded by friends or acquaintances—but not anymore. You can still interact online, stay in touch via Facebook or Twitter, text or call, but it's not the same as when your friends lived right next door and everyone had similar schedules and demands. As great as it was, it will never be like that again.

> I was definitely unprepared for making friends. At school, friends sort of just "hap-pen." You meet people in classes, at clubs, your roommates and their friends, and playing pickup games. But out of school you have to really work for it. People have things to do, and they don't want to leave their apartment.
>
> Joel, 2010

Feeling okay...alone

One of the most important skills you will need to master is the abil-ity to enjoy being alone. There might be some feelings of sadness for those of you who were exceptionally social during college, but all of you will have some level of adjustment to a living environ-ment where you have to make a planned effort to see people. Some of you will be hundreds of miles away from your college friends, and traveling to see each other is just not very feasible.

Although friends are an important part of life at any age, you will soon discover that they are no longer the most important part. As you were growing up, friends helped you understand that you were not alone in the world. This is a significant mes-sage, but it isn't the only message. Your task now is to discover what it means for you to be unique and distinct from the crowd.

Why are you here? What will you contribute during your stay on the planet? That is the question you will be asking and wondering about for this next period of life. Continuing to focus primarily on friends can even be a distraction from this crucial period of exploration, and can keep you tied to self-definitions and perceptions of the past rather than looking toward your future.

Alone but not Lonely

Very often, people equate being alone with loneliness but they are not the same. There are people who have large families, many friends and acquaintances, but still report feeling lonely. In fact, some of you may have felt lonely in college while surrounded by hundreds of others your age.

> In college I knew who I was. Now I realize it was because I had a great group of friends and we had a ton of fun together. Now that I've graduated, I don't have that security anymore. I don't have that group of friends around me every day letting me know I'm important.
>
> Matt, 2010

Loneliness is about being uncomfortable within your own skin not simply an absence of people. It is about feeling not good enough or competent, or worthy, or desirable. Everyone feels this way to some degree or another. It is tempting to think that being with other people can fix these feelings. You may have become dependent upon the distraction provided by the constant activity of a group. But the truth is, staying extremely busy with other people will not help you feel less lonely.

Some people deal with feelings of self-rejection or shyness by staying isolated from people altogether. This, of course, is not the answer either. What we need instead is a balance between productive and focused alone time, and opportunities to connect with others with whom we are free to be ourselves.

Here is the surprising truth: Loneliness can only be fixed by being alone. When you are alone you cannot hide from yourself, and this is the only context where feelings of loneliness can be faced and resolved. Productive time alone is absolutely necessary if you plan on understanding and pursuing those things most important to you.

> *"You need to feel you have safe, peaceful hours when you are free and undisturbed...most creative people need some solitude in order to create...time alone can fuel you, give you vitality and make you more excited about everything."*
> — *Alexandra Stoddard*

Friends will have a place in your life, but not the place they once held, and this transition can sometimes be difficult and sad. In fact, your willingness to participate in this program, to do the work of dreaming and planning, is your first step away from loneliness. You cannot even begin the work if you do not, somewhere down deep, believe you are a person of tremendous value. By beginning this process, you are declaring that you are capable and worthwhile. As you work the plan, mostly in solitude, your feelings of loneliness will begin to subside as your attitude toward yourself improves.

For awhile after college I felt sorry for myself, especially when I read on Facebook about my friends still in school having fun like I used to have. Finally, after a few months, I had to stop reading those posts and start facing my new after college reality.

Brittney, 2008

After you graduate, you may try to stay in touch with your close college friends. Do not be disheartened if you lose contact with some of them. It is hard to keep up with people over long distance. In the beginning, you will feel the loss. But by accepting this new reality as part of your future, and ultimately a good thing, you will begin to move toward the life you've always hoped for. You will find new ways to maintain your closest friendships, but over time, your priorities will begin to shift.

The Benefit of Solitude

During college, being alone was often viewed as a sign of incompetence and failure. No one wanted to sit in their dorm room with the thought that others were out having a good time. But when you like who you are, in spite of the fact that you have areas of needed improvement, you become content with times alone, feeling peaceful and productive. You will still have times with friends, but you won't resent your time alone.

Believe it or not, most people of all ages live with some level of self-rejection. We compensate for this feeling of not being good enough in all the usual ways—distraction, denial, comparison, arrogance, depression, shyness, avoidance, aggression, busyness, etc. But when you can be alone and at peace, you become capable of using your solitude as a tremendous opportunity for awareness, planning, and self-understanding.

There are many uses for solitude, and all of them are important at various times in our lives. Mastering the art of solitude is particularly important for your fifth year because much of the work during this year will happen alone. You need time to think about your dreams, evaluate your plans, and adjust your strategies. The famous writer and spiritual guide Paulo Coelho says this about solitude:

> *Without solitude, no plant or animal can survive, no soil can remain productive for any length of time, no child can learn about life, no artist can create, no work can grow and be transformed.*

Solitude is not the absence of Love, but its complement.

Solitude is not the absence of company, but the moment when our soul is free to speak to us and help us decide what to do with our life.

Therefore, blessed are those who do not fear solitude, who are not afraid of their own company, who are not always desperately looking for something to do, something to amuse themselves with, something to judge.

If you are never alone, you cannot know yourself.[1]

Much of the time our minds are being bombarded by the stimulating and sometimes demanding impressions from the world around us. What we need is the space to allow our inner voices to speak to us and tell us what we really want—to look honestly at what is happening around us, and have the presence of mind to chart a course for action. These thoughts or feelings need to be uncensored, honest, and without refinement. The modifications will come later, but right now you need the freedom to dream.

In college, I can remember feeling comforted by the idea that all around me were people my own age, involved in similar activities and pursuits. Now I live surrounded by people in very different circumstances and settings. It has been a difficult adjustment.

Logan, 2007

So determining your interests and putting those hopes and dreams into a plan will involve significant time alone. Solitude allows your mind to be at rest so it can speak to you. As you quiet the voices of others and listen to the part of you that houses your imagination and true desires, you will discover that which is most authentic to you.

John Jantsch, on his blog, *Duct Tape Marketing*, says this about solitude:

> *Solitude is an intentional step away from every possible distraction. Even folks that work alone suffer from the constant pull of email, phone calls and dozens of online social interactions and distractions. In order to stay true to your business and purpose you must explore ways to create intentional solitude or what I like to call the solo planning practice.*[2]

He outlines several uses for this time alone. First, it is a time to hear yourself—making sure your life is reflecting what you really think and feel. Second, it is a time to get clarity, discovering answers to some of your deepest questions and concerns. Third, a time to "create higher," giving space to allow your creative energies to expand your dreams and desires. Fourth, it is a time to renew purpose, remembering what you want and how your daily life is moving toward your goals and objectives.

> Throughout my years in school, friends came easily from my pool of classmates. Now I needed to develop a new strategy for connecting with others that was more planned out. I wasn't used to thinking about how to make friends or how to be alone. Now I needed to.
>
> **Rachel, 2010**

So practicing solitude allows you to develop a relationship with yourself. Sometimes our culture suggests that being alone is something to avoid or a sign that you aren't living a very exciting life. In college, being with others was usually about having as much fun as possible. Having fun is still important, but you are transitioning out of a time in life when immediate fun is the most important value. Your new focus will be about making plans for your desired future, and if you want to achieve your dreams, you will need to carve out time to make that happen, and much of the work will happen when you are alone.

Don't misunderstand; everyone's dream involves other people in one aspect or another. We talked about the importance of other people in Chapter Four. But no one can define your dream in a way that reflects your real hopes and interests. As we said earlier, knowing what you want only in rough outline form is not enough. Without regular, relaxed solitude you will not have the freedom of mind to work on the specifics of your desired future.

> *"In order to be open to creativity, one must have the capacity for constructive use of solitude. One must overcome the fear of being alone."*
> — *Rollo May*

The Missing Piece

Years ago, I stumbled upon a little book written by Shel Silverstein, called *The Missing Piece Meets the Big O*. It is about relationships but has application to all other endeavors as well.[3]

In the beginning of the story, we are introduced to the Missing Piece (a figure shaped like a slice of pie) who is searching for his perfect match (a circle with a slice missing, just his size)—somebody to help him roll. He goes through many possible options, none of which fit the bill. Finally, after a long search, the Missing Piece finds a perfect fit and for the moment feels happy and complete. But the happiness is short-lived because, unexpectedly, the Missing Piece begins to change and grow until the two pieces aren't fitting together as neatly as before. So they part company, and sadly, the Missing Piece is alone again; disappointed, disheartened and lonely.

Then one day the Missing Piece meets the Big O. He thinks that maybe this is the one he has been waiting for; his perfect fit. However, the Big O explains to the Missing Piece that he isn't missing any pieces and, consequently, there is no place for him to fit. This is confusing for the Missing Piece who can't understand how this is possible. Didn't happiness and fulfillment occur when you finally found someone to help you roll? But the Big O didn't agree and suggests to the Missing Piece that he might try rolling alone.

The Missing Piece had never before heard of such a thing and complains that he isn't designed properly for rolling. He has sharp corners and awkward angles. The Big O explains that corners can smooth down over time and shapes can change with practice. Eventually the Missing Piece decides to give it a try. Slowly, after a bit of effort, he does indeed begin to roll. The final page of the book shows the Missing Piece and the Big O rolling along together, side by side.

Solitude and Relationships

Permit me to take a brief detour to talk about romantic relationships. When most students discuss their future hopes and dreams, they often describe the desire to find a partner they can be with for the rest of their lives. One typical attitude that often hinders a successful future in this regard is this "missing-piece" mentality. They believe that true relational fulfillment will happen when they finally connect with their perfect match.

But so often, just like in Shel Silverstein's book, they are disappointed when the relationship is unable to deliver on the perceived promise of ultimate wholeness. Their well-being is so intertwined with the other person that when growth or change happens, the relationship is put at risk by feelings of panic and anxiety.

> I was more confident about not having a boyfriend when I was in college. Now that I'm out, I am worried about never finding anyone. That thought makes me uncomfortable. It is difficult to see so many of my friends finding partners. I try not to think about it, but sometimes I am filled with worry.
>
> **Mariah, 2009**

Far too often, people assume that all questions will be answered as soon as they find that perfect person. This may be an important aspect of your life goals, but those who believe that personal contentment and satisfaction come magically from a connection with their perfect match will be extremely disillusioned, no matter how loving and faithful their partner might be. Learning to roll on your own is one of the most important preparations for finding relationships that last.

The solitude available in your fifth year is an opportunity to discover the resources for your own happiness and well-being. It is difficult to look into the face of our romance-worshiping culture and say no to the "missing-piece" philosophy of life. Even if you believe that meeting your long-term partner is way down the road, you can still be adversely affected by the misconception that someday your "missing piece" will roll by and you will become magically whole.

Whether or not you are currently in a relationship, the liminal period provides a great opportunity to practice taking responsibility for your own feelings of security, contentment, and fullness—a skill you will work on throughout your life. This is without question the best preparation for the day you meet your Big O and decide to make a commitment to someone with whom you can enjoy rolling side by side.

Isolation Therapy

Find five activities that you usually do with other people and do them alone. Record in your journal how the experience made you feel. Add to the list below.

1. Go to a movie you really wanted to see.

2. Take yourself to dinner and bring a book with you to read.

3. Attend a free concert at a park or coffee shop.

4. Attend a sporting event.

Knowing that you can be happy alone is one of the most important preparations for a good relationship. You don't necessarily need to be single to learn this, but it is one of the many additional benefits to the liminal period, when there may be some long stretches of time without "someone special" in your life. Being "unattached" and taking time for solitude can be one of the best ways to practice the art of becoming less needy and more self-sufficient.

I am not advocating isolation or withdrawal, but I am saying that neediness, self-rejection, and insecurity are not trustworthy motivations leading to success or happiness in your relationships or your life. This is a time to become comfortable in your own skin and discover a contentment that is not dependent on the attention of others.

Practice Solitude

So it is time to make a decision to not run from solitude. Since we are all different, no one should feel forced to be alone in the same way as others. You may have some anxiety at first when you are home by yourself and you're convinced everyone else is "out there" having a good time. Especially when you get on Facebook and believe that people are as exciting as their pictures seem to suggest. It is time to move on to other matters that will affect your future contentment more than just another night of hanging out with friends.

Enjoying Solitude

There are many activities that are fit for doing alone. Sometimes we avoid these because we are afraid of the quietness. Make a list of activities you might enjoy doing alone. Include one or two of these in your schedule every week. Here are some examples:

1. Regularly go on a bike ride.

2. Take a walk.

3. Read a book.

4. Learn a new musical instrument.

5. Take up gardening.

6. Visit an art museum.

7. Sit on a park bench for 30 minutes.

Living the life you want takes work and much of that work will be done apart from the crowd. Becoming comfortable with who you are through your time alone is necessary to discover what you are hoping for in your life. No one will just walk up and hand it to you because you are a nice person. It won't be easy even if you are a genius or have amazing talent.

If you were to ask me which is more important, having great talent or having an amazing ability to work hard and persevere, I would pick the drive every time. If you look at the successful people around you, most of them got there by working hard at something over a long period of time, no matter how much talent they possessed. I guarantee that what looks like talent now, started out as effort, planning, and persistence. Much of this energy comes from within; qualities you will discover and explore in solitude. So don't fight it. Solitude is the rich soil in which this energy and commitment grows best. Give it a chance. Block out the noise and find out more about what you love to do, what you find meaningful and fulfilling, and where you want to go in life.

> *"Creativity is essentially a lonely art. An even lonelier struggle. To some a blessing. To others a curse. It is in reality the ability to reach inside yourself and drag forth from your very soul an idea."*
> *— Lou Dorfsman*

REMEMBER

❖ Your task is to discover what it means to be unique and distinct from the crowd.

❖ Continuing to focus primarily on friends can be a distraction from this crucial period of exploration, and can keep you tied to the self-definitions and perceptions of the past rather than looking toward your future.

❖ Loneliness can only be fixed by being alone.

❖ The solitude available in your fifth year is an opportunity to discover the resources for your own happiness and well-being.

❖ If you want to achieve your dreams, you will need to carve out time to make that happen, and most of the work will happen when you are alone.

❖ Your liminal period can be a time to become comfortable in your own skin and discover a contentment that is not dependent on the attention of others.

CHAPTER NINE

CONFRONT FEAR

*Courage is not the absence of fear, but the willingness
to press ahead and take action in the face of it.*

*"Courage is being scared to death... and saddling
up anyway."*
                                    — *John Wayne*

I n 1819, the 238 ton whale ship Essex set sail from Nantucket
Island on a routine voyage hunting for whales. Before electricity, whales were hunted almost to the point of extinction
because whale oil was the primary fuel used in oil lamps, the
main source of lighting throughout the world. After a long fifteen months at sea, the Essex was thousands of miles off the
Western coast of South America when a pod of whales was
spotted. The two smaller whaling boats were lowered into the
water and the hunt was on. Captain Pollard was in one boat
and Owen Chase, the first mate, in the other. Chase struck the

first blow with his harpoon, but his little boat received some damage and he was forced to return to the Essex for repairs. It was then that the unthinkable happened.

Back on the Essex, Chase was assessing the damage to his smaller boat, and saw a large white whale some distance off the port bow. He thought it strange that the whale was just sitting there, motionless, and spouting. Suddenly the whale, which Chase estimated to be about eighty-five feet in length, dove under the water. To Chase's astonishment, the whale surfaced and was headed straight for the *Essex*. Chase yelled out to the helmsman to turn the ship but it was too late. He wrote later in his narrative of the event, "He gave us such an appalling and tremendous jar, as nearly threw us all on our faces." He said that the crew was stunned at what had just happened. Nothing like this had ever been reported before.

But it was not over. The whale lay off the ship a short distance, also stunned, but not for long. Soon, Chase writes, "He was enveloped in the foam of the sea that his continued and violent thrashing about in the water had created around him. I could distinctly see him smite his jaws together, as if distracted with rage and fury." Suddenly, he heard someone cry, "Here he is again-he is making for us again" Chase turned around and saw the whale heading directly for the *Essex*, this time with a re-newed fury. Chase wrote that the whale was bearing down on them at twice the normal speed. The great white whale once again crashed into the ship, this time the *Essex* was doomed. Chase wrote, "He struck her to windward, directly under the cat-head, and completely stove in her bows." The whale passed under the ship never to be seen again.

The men were forced to abandon the Essex and were now adrift in the three smaller whaling boats. They were hundreds of miles from the nearest land in the biggest ocean in the world. Herman Melville would use this dramatic tale as inspiration for his epic novel, Moby Dick.

While stranded in the water the crew needed to make a plan for their survival. Imagine the fear that must have been gripping these twenty-one men, many of them in their early twenties. They had three options. The closest known island, Tahiti, was more than twelve hundred miles to the west but the crew had heard rumors that it was inhabited by cannibals. Another choice was Hawaii, but being storm season, they assumed this direction would also lead to catastrophe. Their final possibility was the longest and the most difficult. Sail south for a thousand miles before they could use the Westerlies to turn towards Peru, which would still lie another three thousand miles to the east. However, their food and water made this option at least as bad as the others. So they had a decision to make; be eaten by cannibals, capsize and drown in a storm, or die of starvation. They ended up choosing the longest route, and consequently, most of the men did starve. Only five of the sailors lived to tell the story.[1]

Melville would later say that had they chosen one of the other two routes, there was a good chance all would have survived since stories of cannibalism were often exaggerated or mythical, and killer storms were intermittent at best.[2] So, what caused the men to choose the route they did? Only one answer makes sense. The sailors were more afraid of cannibals and storms than they were of starvation. The vividness of being eaten by cannibals or being crushed in a violent storm felt more threatening than the more subtle dangers of dehydration and starvation.

Our fears will affect our decisions as much as our opportunities, and they can fool us. We often choose to avoid our most dramatic or vivid fears while not paying attention to the most dangerous ones. The fact was: Starvation was a much more likely scenario for these crew members than being eaten by cannibals or destroyed in a violent storm, but no one at the time could see it. Their fearful imaginations of cannibals and storms skewed their judgment.

Facing the unknown is scary. Nothing has more debilitating or disruptive potential than the experience of fear. The truth is, we are all afraid, and recognizing its presence is the first step in getting past it. Fear is at the source of our resistance, the reason for our hesitation and the brake pedal on our progress.

Whatever you do in your life, you will do it in the face of fear. Thinking there will be a time when you are not afraid, or worse still, thinking that you will accomplish something after fear has been defeated, is a recipe for paralysis. Fear is a part of our humanity; it operates in an effort to keep us safe and protected in a world of danger. Unfortunately, fear also holds us back when we should press ahead. Since there are so many threats in the world, this instinct for safety works to keep us alive, but fear doesn't discriminate between something to be avoided or something to be overcome.

> I am unprepared for this feeling of not knowing what's going to happen. All the way through college, I have had my way planned. Now it all feels so uncertain. The uncertainty is overwhelming.
>
> Mark, 2007

Parents understand this. When you have a child, your obvious instinct is to protect them. That protection instinct is not tempered by logic. Parents grow accustomed to living at all times with this feeling of caution in regard to their young children, and later, it is the reason they are restless and irritable until their teenagers are home safe in their beds. How many times can you remember coming home late, only to find your mom or dad waiting up for you, asking, "Where have you been? Why are you so late?" It sounded intrusive and nosy, but what you were hearing was the voice of fear.

The Unpredictable World

We live in an uncertain and unpredictable world, where anything can happen. This is both a blessing and a curse. The goal is not to eliminate fear from your life or even eliminate unnecessary fears. You are not defective if you have fears about things that are not threatening. As I said, fear is neither intelligent nor discriminating. Fear is here to stay, so we must renegotiate our relationship to it, expecting it to show up, and finding strategies for action in spite of it.

Some time ago, Sue and I decided to make a move from Southern California, where we grew up, to Arkansas. We had three small children at the time and the move was the culmination of a long process of evaluating, researching, and planning for our next move. Siloam Springs is a small town in Northwest Arkansas with a total population of twelve-thousand people. I'm a little embarrassed to admit that when I first received a call to consider this move, I had to grab an atlas to pinpoint its location. Most native Californians at that time (at least these two) had a hard time picturing the exact position of any states east of Nevada. The most common reaction I received from friends and family when I told them of our decision to move to Arkansas was: "Why?"

For several years, I had developed a dream to work on a college campus and participate in the growing up process of young adults. In addition to this, Sue and I often talked about our desire to live in another part of the country and in a smaller town. I researched college and universities in the United States and ended up sending over two-hundred personal letters to the presidents of these schools asking for a job. After describing my background and experience, I asked them to contact me if they had any job openings where I might fit. Throughout that year, I received encouraging and supportive responses to almost all those letters, stating that "although we believe you would be a tremendous asset at our college, we simply have no openings for you at this time." Most of them said they would keep my name on file in case anything changed in the near future. I wasn't holding my breath. I admit it wasn't a great plan, but it was the plan I acted upon.

Almost a year later, I actually received a call from one of these colleges wondering if I was still interested in working on a campus. Over the course of the next few months, I interviewed for the job, made two visits to the campus, and was ultimately hired. It is hard to put into words the differences between Los Angeles, CA and Siloam Springs, AR. At the time, this decision to move from our home town, our families and friends, and everything that was familiar, was mostly a move into the unknown. I can remember long hours of conversation, the pros and cons lists, travel books, and efforts to picture what life would be like in small town Arkansas. But nothing would take away our feelings of uncertainty and hesitation in making this life-changing decision. I can remember that feeling of reluctance we had, and the choice between a fairly specific desire and opportunity, and the much safer decision to take a different, non-campus job, much closer to home.

When you are reaching toward your dreams, you will often come to the place when you must act in the face of the fear, uncertainty, and doubt. Choosing to stay close to home would not necessarily equate with missing out on my dreams, but doing so simply because I was afraid of the unknown, would have placed an unfortunate limitation on finding the life I wanted.

Our decision to move to Arkansas from California brought a variety of unexpected adjustments and surprises. But it also brought some amazing opportunities, memories, and lifelong friendships that continue to enrich our lives to this day.

Most of you have already made many decisions to move forward in life in spite of feeling uncertain or unclear about what was in store. Some of you may have felt some level of fear and hesitation when you chose to leave home and go to college. But think about what made that decision a little easier than the decisions and fears you are now facing as a graduate. Although the decision to go to college was truly a move into the unknown, it was not completely unfamiliar to you. Siblings or friends, who had gone to college, possibly even to the college you were planning to attend, were planning to attend, provided some understanding about college life. When I ask students why they chose to attend our particular college, often they say they had a parent, relative or friend who had attended years before. They were able to gain some sense about what the campus experience would be like which helped moderate their fears and expectations.

> The difficult part of graduating from college was knowing so little about my next step. Many of my friends were going to graduate school but that wasn't for me. School was all I had known. What came next felt like a dark hole.
>
> **Jeremy, 2008**

One of the most challenging aspects of the twenty-something liminal experience in our modern culture is the lack of knowledgeable guides who have already traveled through the uncertainties and unknowns of this period of life. There may come a time when the post-college life is less ambiguous and vague because the experience will be so well documented and understood. But for now, emerging adults not only face uncertainty, they also cannot consult previous generations for information and guidance.

Less Control, More Fear

Ambiguity cannot be avoided during these years especially when you are working hard to discover and live your dreams. We do not live in a predictable or static world where we can easily or confidently determine the outcome of every decision we make. First of all, we are not in charge of everything that affects us. Earlier I emphasized that discovering and living your dreams is completely within your power to accomplish, which is true. I also said, however, that you must remain flexible with your approaches because many things, outside of you, are not in your control. Not only are natural laws unpredictable such as hurricanes, tornados, floods and earthquakes, but the choices other people make are unpredictable as well. When terrorists flew planes into the World Trade Center on September 11, 2001, we had nothing to do with that decision, and yet it affected all of our lives.

One recent summer in Virginia, we were on a hurricane watch when all of a sudden, with no warning, we had an earthquake. That's how life goes sometimes. Fear is the defensive instinct that prepares us to react to unexpected or threatening events. Without the instinct of fear, we may walk in front of moving vehicles, fall off cliffs, or get mugged regularly in dark alleys. We live in an unpredictable world that requires us to be prepared for anything. Expecting it to be different is a waste of time. Rather than hoping to do away with fear, we must be prepared to feel it, evaluate it, and often, take action in spite of it.

Uncertainty is Bitter Sweet

We love and hate the random and uncertain nature of life. We love unpredictability because it makes life exciting and invigorating. Anything can happen. And more to the point, we can be a part of making that "anything" happen. But it can also make life feel threatening and scary.

Creating the life you want and achieving your dreams depends upon believing that your decisions and actions can change the world. When we don't believe this is the case, we become depressed, discouraged, and lose motivation. That is one of the many faces fear wears. We might say to ourselves, "Who am I kidding? What difference does it make? I can't change things." That is the voice of fear.

Accepting that life is unpredictable can generate feelings of hopefulness. We boldly fly into the face of fear when we choose to believe that anything is possible. Therefore, fear will feel the strongest when we are living close to the unpredictable nature of life, and especially when we are trying to make significant changes in our experience.

When we are resigned to living the life we have been assigned, simply going through the motions and accepting the way things are, feelings of fear lessen. We feel no fear because we are living as if we have no power to influence our experience. Life feels predictable, even though it may be predictably bad. We accept that our life is the way it is as a matter of fate, and we choose to simply embrace it and make the best of it. Fear has no obvious presence when we live this way. If we encounter a new opportunity or relationship, we detect fear and quickly move to shut it down.

But when we recognize that this is not the world we live in, not the truth about life; that this planet is not predictable, and that our thoughts and actions do have the power to change things, then we have just invited fear to the party. So my message to you is simple: open the door to fear. Swing it wide open and welcome it in. It is telling you something important. It means you are embracing life as it really is, and not settling for a fake, protected, predictable way of seeing your world and living in it.

Too many people resign themselves to living fear-free by avoiding uncertainty and adventure at all costs. Don't be one of them.

Don't let fear keep you from reaching for the life you want; one that is full of options and opportunity. We all need a measure of safety and security in our lives, but don't let the anticipation or presence of fear dissuade you from pursuing your dreams.

Often fear is viewed as a negative emotion, one to eradicate as quickly as possible. But if we live afraid of fear, we shrink away from the possibilities that can move us toward the life we desire.

No Fear, No Future

How did early explorers have the courage to strike out in search of a new world or a great treasure? What motivated the American pioneers to leave the security of the city, jump on rickety horse-pulled wagons, and head west into danger and the unknown? Maybe they weren't conditioned by years of training to choose security over risk. For us today, choosing risk seems foolish.

> Who knew the early twenties would be such a struggle? On one hand, everything is at your fingertips and you have the power to choose your life's course and there is little to hold you back. You're in your prime and you're young and free. But who knew 'the best time of my life' would be so scary?
>
> Joel, 2009

We are taught to value security and predictability over freedom. We are trained to never draw outside the lines, not value individual initiative or creativity. And consequently, our instinct is to avoid fear at all costs. If we try to express our unique interests, abilities, or thoughts, we receive either a verbal slap on the wrist by our teachers for not providing the "right" answer, or ridicule by our peers for standing out and being "different".

Our progress and growth demand that we act in spite of fear. It takes courage in the face of fear to confront your past and resolve former hurts. It takes courage to be open about your weaknesses and limitations and do something about them. It takes courage to honestly acknowledge and learn from your mistakes. It takes courage to confess and articulate your dreams and make plans to move toward them. It is much easier to live in denial or avoidance, rather than do what is necessary to live the life you desire.

Fear verses Boredom

For years, we have been taught to associate "not fitting in" with failure and so we fear it. But fear is not an enemy any more than pain is an enemy. They are simply warning signals. They alert you to pay attention. If you feel afraid because of an oncoming train, then by all means, get out of the way. But if the fear is because you are trying something challenging, distinctive, or new, then take note, pay attention, and press ahead.

Also, take notice of those times when you do not feel fear. Are you settling into predictability and security, avoiding risk by simply following directions and obeying the rules? That would be a time to revisit your dreams and check your strategy. Is fear holding you back? Have you settled for something less than what you want?

Maybe one of the reasons the party culture is so extreme in colleges and universities today is because of the predictability and powerlessness students often feel within the college world. People who are bent on finding and living their dreams have less time and interest in escaping. They are too excited and engrossed in the road they are on; why would they ever want to escape it?

A good book outlining the escapist tendencies on college campuses is *Binge* by Barrett Seaman. Seaman, a former Time Magazine Reporter, and White House Correspondent and Editor, visited twelve college campuses across the country. He lived in student housing, and wrote about the life he witnessed there. He provides a good picture of the extent of escapism prevalent on the typical university campus.[3] Some people view this as a positive thing—sowing your wild oats, enjoying your youth, the last hurrah before adulthood, etc. However, I think it's what happens when you take energetic, enthusiastic and passionate young people and tell them to sit still, pay attention, follow the catalogue or syllabus, and do what they're told. They get restless and frustrated just as they should. Where did they get the notion that "real" life is dull, so you better "live it up" while you are young?

> I am a recent graduate and I am trying to live it up as much as possible while I'm young. I'm traveling, exploring and having fun now, because pretty soon I'll have to settle down and get serious.
>
> Bridget, 2011

Although there are exceptions, I've discovered that most college students are bored with school. They are young, curious, motivated, energetic, and excited, but many parts of the educational system often fail to explore and support those amazing qualities. Students will seek to escape whenever possible when no avenues seem available for these impulses. It is not within their DNA to accept security and predictability at the cost of losing their individuality, creativity, and freedom.

Some time ago, I was involved with the beginning of a new student movement on the campus where I worked. It started with the passion and efforts of one student and spread to hundreds of others in a very short time. I began to notice something among the students who became a part of this movement. They weren't bored. There was something going on inside them that changed their attitude about their lives. They could still have fun together, but they were no longer escaping. They felt important and needed and nothing in their academic curriculum could match the enthusiasm generated by their lofty ideals and plans to help others in a developing country.

This organization has been in existence for nearly ten years now and still provides tremendous opportunity and vitality to students who get involved. They raise money for amazing projects, travel overseas to build schools and orphanages, and have already altered the living conditions for hundreds of children and families. Most of these students do so because the work makes them feel vital and empowered. It taps into something basic about being human. We all want our lives to count; to make a difference in the world, but it cannot happen without a willingness to get outside our comfort zones. Predictability and security are not reliable guides for discovering the meaning and purpose all humans seek.

I am not suggesting that we will always feel energized and excited about our dreams or strategies. Clearly, there are tedious times in all worthy projects and plans. But this is different than the dullness that comes from feeling powerless, predictable, or bored. Staying close to your dreams and paying attention to your plans even in the face of the unknown is the way to remain energized and alert in a world that needs your passion, participation, and ideas. Don't just settle for the most certain or guaranteed.

Amanda, a recent graduate, called me to say that she quit her job. It was a good job; one that she had trained for in college, but it no longer fit her growing dream for her life. She decided to take a leap and explore her passion of working in another country with an organization that helps underprivileged children. Most people would consider this choice unwise or too risky. But if it moves

Amanda toward her dream, and she is honest about the challenges, not making the move might be the more risky decision.

This is not to suggest that you stop the job hunt, or that you quit yours if you have one. However, if you settle for nothing more than the security of having a job, you may miss out on what you really want to do with your life. Thinking that there will come a day when you will no longer need to face feelings of fear, or act courageously, is to suggest that there will come a day when life is no longer an adventure. And why would any of us ever wish for that?

Protection and Fear

Joseph LeDoux, professor of neural science and psychology at New York University, is also the director of the Emotional Brain Institute. He has done extensive research and writing on the topic of fear. He says,

> Every animal (including insects and worms, as well as animals more like us) is born with the ability to detect and respond to certain kinds of danger, and to learn about things associated with risk. In short, the capacity to fear (in the sense of detecting and responding to danger) is pretty universal among animals.[4]

He goes on to say that anxiety about this fear is enhanced among humans because of our ability to envision and anticipate the future. Therefore, we are able to not only protect ourselves in the present, we are also able to protect ourselves from things well into the future.

> While anxiety is defined by uncertainty, human anxiety is greatly amplified by our ability to imagine the future, and our place in it, even a future that is physically impossible. With imagination we can ruminate over that

yet to be experienced, possibly impossible, scenario. We use this creative capacity to great advantage when we envision how to make our lives better, but we can just as easily put it to work in less productive ways— worrying excessively about the outcome of things.[5]

We have given up too much in order to escape from the uncomfortable feelings associated with fear and anxiety. We have lost our relationship with the uncertain, unpredictable world, and in its place we sometimes settle for safe, protected, secure, dull, and boring. This tendency is especially harmful to you, those at the beginning of your journey. At this point in your life, there is no good reason to avoid adventure, exploration, or risk. Instead, reach for the life you desire.

> *"All happiness depends on courage and work."*
> *— Honoré de Balzac*

Overcoming Fear

Begin a list of all the things you are afraid will happen if you pursue your dreams. Pick one of these and pretend it happened. Make a plan of what you might do if the worst happened.

1. I am afraid of not having enough money to support myself.

2. I am afraid of getting into something I don't like doing.

3. I am afraid of looking foolish.

4. I am afraid of not being able to finish the job.

Finding the life you want will demand that you develop a more positive relationship with fear. If you begin to move down these paths, you will discover many reasons to not press forward into your real interests and passions. Fear is not simply being scared. It is resistance. It tells you, in no uncertain terms, that you are crazy to think you can live the life you want or do the things you want to do. In fact, you will be tempted to give up even before you know what your dream actually is.

Fear is trying to protect you, so it may swing into operation even before your desires are clearly formulated. It will tell you to "stop being silly," and "things like that don't happen to people like you." That is fear talking. So tell yourself, "be calm." "I am not deciding to do anything yet." Be prepared for fear as you do this work. Expect it. Look for it, name it, and then act in spite of it.

> *"Inaction breeds doubt and fear. Action breeds confidence and courage. If you want to conquer fear, do not sit home and think about it. Go out and get busy."*
>
> — *Dale Carnegie*

REMEMBER

❖ When you are reaching forward toward your dreams, you will often come to the place when you must act in the face of the fear and the uncertainty.

❖ Thinking there will be a time when we are not afraid, or worse still, thinking that we will accomplish something after we have defeated fear, is a recipe for paralysis.

❖ Creating the life you want and achieving your dreams depends upon believing that life invites your participation and you can actually make decisions that change the world.

❖ If the fear is because we are trying something unique or challenging and might fail, then we take note, pay attention, and press ahead.

❖ We all want our lives to count; to make a difference in the world, but it cannot happen without a willingness to get outside of our comfort zone.

.

CHAPTER TEN

EXCERCISE GRATITUDE

How do we stay awake to the undeniable truth and amazing reality that we are all alive in the here and now, and are having the incredible experience of living in this astounding and miraculous world?

"The essence of all beautiful art, all great art, is gratitude."

— *Friedrich Nietzsche*

Recently, I was in an airplane headed to Mammoth Lakes, California, to spend a few days in the snow with friends and family. It was an hour flight that left Los Angeles at 3:45 p.m. and was scheduled to land at 5:00 p.m. With about ten minutes to go before landing, the pilot made an announcement: "For those of you on the left side of the airplane, if you look out the window, you will see one of the reasons I love flying this particular route."

I happened to be sitting on that side of the plane, so I looked out the window at one of the most beautiful sunsets I had ever seen. The colors in the sky were stunning as the sun dropped below the snow-covered peaks in the distance. The entire plane full of people became quiet as everyone took a moment to enjoy the amazing sight—it was remarkable.

While watching a colorful sunset, like I did that day, or sitting mesmerized by the rolling waves on a beautiful beach, I often think about how many times that sight has occurred throughout history. For hundreds of years, people have watched and enjoyed the same miracle of colors and beauty.

Don't you wonder what these people from the past might have been doing or thinking about during their moment in the sun? I assume they had dreams, hopes and hurts just like we do now. And someday in the future, long after we are gone, there will be someone else looking into the sky, enjoying the beauty, and possibly thinking about us.

Were these people of the past happy, discouraged, frustrated, hurt, lost, or just taking a break from their duties and dreams? Did this moment of gazing help them see the world differently or did they quickly look away and get on with their day? Did they take a moment to feel grateful for the eyes to see it or the good fortune to be outdoors?

Sometimes these beautiful sights in nature can cause us to feel a measure of gratitude for being alive. This attitude of gratefulness plays an important role in pursuing of the life we desire.

"Gratitude bestows reverence, allowing us to encounter everyday epiphanies, those transcendent moments of awe that change forever how we experience life and the world."

— *John Milton*

Gratitude and Contentment

The following poem was written by child psychologist David L. Weatherford. It should make all of us take a moment and consider our perspective on life.

Have you ever watched kids on a merry-go-round?
Or listened to the rain slapping on the ground?

Ever followed a butterfly's erratic flight,
or gazed at the sun into the fading night?

You better slow down. Don't dance so fast.
Time is short. The music won't last.

Do you run through each day on the fly?
When you ask: how are you? Do you hear the reply?

When the day is done, do you lie in your bed?
With the next hundred chores running through your head?

You'd better slow down. Don't dance so fast.
Time is short. The music won't last.

Ever told your child, we'll do it tomorrow?
And in your haste, not see his sorrow?

Ever lost touch, let a friendship die
Cause you never had time to call and say, Hi.

You'd better slow down. Don't dance so fast.
Time is short. The Music won't last.

When you run so fast to get somewhere
you miss half the fun of getting there.

When you worry and hurry through your day,
it is like an unopened gift thrown away.

Life is not a race. Do take it slower.
Hear the music, before the song is over.[1]

Exercising gratitude is a mental practice that will serve you well throughout the rest of your life. We may think gratitude only occurs spontaneously when good things happen. Gratitude happens at these moments because we are jolted into seeing an aspect of reality that normally stays hidden from our view. There is an important connection between our happiness and our ability to be grateful.

How do we stay awake to the undeniable truth and amazing reality that we are all alive in the here and now, and are having the incredible experience of living in this astounding and miraculous world?

"Gratitude unlocks the fullness of life. It turns what we have into enough, and more. It turns denial into acceptance, chaos to order, confusion to clarity. It can turn a meal into a feast, a house into a home, a stranger into a friend."

— Melody Beattie

Gratitude and Humility

Gratitude is about living with humility. Having a sense that someday my time will be over and I'll, literally and figuratively, be history. This is my time to make the most of life and live with purpose, resolve, and joy. People who live with gratitude are definitely not the only people who accomplish important work and make a difference in the world. But only grateful people seem to enjoy it. Without gratitude there is no happiness.

One of my favorite conversations about gratitude occurs in the movie *Joe Versus the Volcano*. Joe and Patricia are on the ocean, in her father's boat. Joe looks up at the stars and expresses his wonder at the beauty and expanse of the sky and the brightness of the stars.

He looks at her and asks, "Do you believe in God?"

She answers, "I believe in myself."

"What does that mean?" he continues.

She says, "It means I have confidence in myself."

Joe thinks for a moment and then says, "You know, I've done a lot of soul searching lately. I've been asking myself some pretty tough questions. You know what I've found out? I have no interest in myself. I think about myself and I get bored out of my mind."

Then, after a short pause, Patricia makes this comment: "My father says that almost the whole world is asleep. Everybody you know. Everybody you see. Everybody you talk to. He says that only a few people are awake, and they live in a state of constant, total amazement."[2]

Gratitude is a habit. It is the way of living in constant, total amazement. It is not simply the practice of saying "thank you" as if someone just passed you the salt at dinner. Gratitude is a way of seeing the world not only as half full, but as mostly full. And here is the good news; it is not a talent you needed to be born with. It is a skill you can practice.

> *"Our goal should be to live life in radical amazement. ....get up in the morning and look at the world in a way that takes nothing for granted. Everything is phenomenal; everything is incredible; never treat life casually. To be spiritual is to be amazed."*
> — *Abraham Joshua Heschel*

Gratitude as a State of Mind

Gratitude is a state of mind that can prevent you from missing out on the amazing reality of being alive right now in this moment of history. It is an acquired skill that pulls you into the present moment. Pursuing your dreams is not selfish, it is stewardship. It is taking this amazing gift of being alive and learning to embrace it and fully live it as authentically and consistently as humanly possible.

You can waste a lot of time and energy trying to escape from the difficult aspects of your life, or the grind of day-to-day living. But is that really all we desire? Somewhere down deep, most of us want to discover a kind of living that is full of amazement, wonder and meaning, from which we feel no need to escape.

A speaker I once heard defined gratitude as "feeling blessed." Blessing is not a word we hear often in daily conversation, but its meaning is very close to gratitude. He described blessed as "feeling lucky." When we feel lucky or fortunate we are experiencing the emotion of gratitude.

So in this following exercise, I want you to begin a lucky list. Add to it each day as you think of new items that make you a fortunate person. You may not feel differently at first, but don't worry about that; just make the list. Each one of you can put at the top of your list that you are alive, and you can read. Each of us should be able to fill up at least a page of items in only a few minutes.

But keep it going throughout the month and watch how it will begin to alter your feelings about your life and your circumstances. As you continue down your list think carefully about each item and how different life would be without it. Put this list up on a wall or on a mirror where you pass by each day. Stop and read the list every few days to remember why you are such a fortunate person. People who feel lucky, feel happy.

> *"The privilege of a lifetime is being who you are."*
> — *Joseph Campbell*

Your Lucky List (try to be very specific)
Write 3 new items each day for 30 days

1. The Starbucks barista remembered my order.

2. I'm grateful for the good book I'm reading right now.

3. My mom just sent me a batch of my favorite cookies.

4. One of my best friends from college sent me a text just to say hello.

5. I spent time yesterday just listing to the birds sing.

6. I live close enough to work to walk and enjoy the morning.

7. I had a lunch with a good friend yesterday and we laughed a lot.

8. I have a job that allows me to make a difference in other people's lives.

Living in gratitude is the bedrock of happiness, and happiness is the direct by-product of gratitude. Gratitude is what we experience when we are feeling happy. You cannot practice happiness but you can practice gratitude which creates happy and pleasant feelings. Happiness could be easily defined as a grateful state of mind. Again, we think we have no control over this. We believe that circumstances dictate whether or not we have this happy/grateful feeling. But this is not correct.

In September 1998, Michael J. Fox, at thirty years of age, announced to the world that he had been diagnosed with Parkinson's disease, a degenerative neurological condition usually found in people much older. By then, he had been secretly fighting it for several years, yet by the time the world found out, he had come to terms with the diagnosis. So as the public started grieving for him, he had stopped grieving for himself.

In his memoir, written in 2002, he recounts his life from his childhood in a small town in western Canada, to his meteoric rise in film and television which made him a worldwide celebrity. Most importantly however, he writes of the last ten years, during which, with the unswerving support of his wife, family, and friends, he has dealt with his illness. He talks about what Parkinson's has given him: the chance to appreciate a wonderful life and career, and the opportunity to help search for a cure and spread public awareness of the disease. The title of his book is "Lucky Man."[3]

Gratitude and Circumstances

I am not claiming that gratitude is a magical solution to all our problems. However, I am saying that no matter what happens to us, we can take responsibility for the way we feel and think. That is the game changer. This is why people who are going through difficult circumstances, like Michael J. Fox, can often feel very happy, while others with extreme comforts and privileges can sometimes be so miserable.

The difference is gratitude, a mental state that remains amazed at the world and aware of good fortune, no matter what the circumstances or conditions may be at any given moment. Sometimes the more that goes our way, the more we expect things to go our way. This is what people mean when they talk about feelings of entitlement. We come to expect, or feel like we deserve a problem-free life. So the slightest hiccup can send us into a tailspin. Clearly, many of our difficulties are far more serious than a hiccup, but often suffering causes us to pause in our lives, re-order our thinking, and remember all the reasons (our lucky list) to feel grateful and blessed in spite of our problems. We begin to notice and appreciate things that we had taken for granted.

My first two grandchildren were born this past summer. I loved it when my own children were born. Those four births are my best memories. But at that time in my life I was also wrapped up in the process of caring for them and, working with my wife Sue, to make a life for them. With my grandchildren, I have none of those responsibilities, which means I am happily left to simply watch and wonder at the miracle of these two little people showing up in the world and beginning to find their way around. It feels like my potential for enjoyment went into overdrive. There is a relaxed and peaceful gratitude that no words can express.

We live in a world that often doesn't value these "do nothing" watchful moments, but they can remind us that our lives are more than what we do. Our many "doings" can sometimes cause us to lose the sense of wonder, amazement, and sheer happiness in our "being." We are concentrating so hard on what we are doing that we do not take the time for moments of observation, astonishment, and surprise.

John Muir lived his life for the outdoors. He was passionate about the preservation of natural beauty in the American wilderness. He was the inspiration for Theodore Roosevelt's efforts to set aside and protect vast acres of land throughout the United States, including Yosemite and Sequoia, in the National Parks project. He once said:

Everybody needs beauty as well as bread, places to play in and pray in, where nature may heal and give strength to body and soul. Thousands of tired, nerve-shaken,

over-civilized people are beginning to find out that go-
ing to the mountains is going home; that wilderness is
a necessity; and that mountain parks and reservations
are useful not only as fountains of timber and irrigating
rivers, but as fountains of life.[4]

Question your approach to living if there is no room for periods of astonishment and wonder. This will take more work for some than for others. Some of you already have a practice of doing this in your life, but others will need more guidance and help. Again, let me remind you, gratitude is about a way of seeing the world, and not simply the result of positive or happy conditions.

The following exercise will give you a way to practice gratitude. We can become accustomed to complaining and negativity when bad things happen, but to stay in that state for too long is to miss out on everything else going on. At any given moment, each of us could potentially list many things not going well. Life usually does not move forward in a straight line.

Gratitude is a mentality that refuses to believe that the bad circumstances are the whole story. In order to maintain emotional balance, we must practice seeing more than just the misfortune. Unfortunately, trouble is very loud and demanding. Practicing gratitude will help you maintain your resolve and positive outlook in the face of frustrations and hardship.

The following exercise will challenge you to practice seeing more than just the problems in your life circumstances. When problems come into your life, as they inevitably will, you will need a way to keep your perspective and not lose your footing.

Practicing Gratitude in Difficult Circumstances

Make a list of all the events or circumstances in your life that are causing you to be upset or unhappy. Fully explain the situation and how it makes you feel. After each one, make a list of four or five things you can be grateful about in each circumstance in spite of the frustration. Read this list aloud every morning for seven days.

Example:

1. I am not making enough money at my job to pay my bills and this causes me to feel hopeless and discouraged.

   a. I am grateful because I have a job and I can pay some of my bills.

   b. I am grateful because I have parents willing to let me stay with them for awhile.

   c. I am grateful that I am healthy enough to work and I can look for another job.

   d. I am grateful for some good friends who support me and encourage me.

   e. I am grateful for the time to think about what I really want to do.

Most of this book revolves around important aspects of your future—knowing and living your dreams. But your capacity to focus properly on your future depends, to a great degree, on your ability to live in and be grateful for your present. If you assume that happiness is something you will experience someday when certain things happen, then you will not only slow down your progress, you will also risk being disillusioned when you reach your goals.

In graduate school, I became friends with the baseball coach at the college I was attending. That year, his team won the NCAA College Division 1 World Series in Omaha, Nebraska. When I congratulated him on this career-making accomplishment, he responded in an unexpected way. He told me that the day he stood near the pitcher's mound and received the trophy signifying that his team was the best college baseball team in the country was the emptiest day of his life!

He went on to explain that this dream had been the driving force of his life for many, many years. Nothing was more important to him than winning this championship and trophy. It was his life goal as a coach. He sacrificed much in order to reach this goal, but when it finally happened, it didn't provide the happiness or fulfillment he expected. He had focused so much on the future that he never developed the practice of enjoying the process of getting there.

This is not a unique story. Often, people who have this experience, deal with the emptiness by quickly beginning another pursuit for yet another distant goal. Rarely, however, do they question their approach to achieving contentment. In the end, they accomplish much but experience little true satisfaction. Only our efforts at gratitude will change this scenario.

Accomplishing great things will only feel great if it provides us with the sense of peace and fulfillment we seek. Your efforts at knowing and achieving your dream are a huge part of finding the life you want. But your ability to be amazed at the world, maintain gratitude in the face of difficulty and see more than just misfortune will have a direct correlation with your ability to truly enjoy reaching your goals. All of us must learn and practice being grateful, no matter what is happening day by day.

Gratitude and Service

One of the many ways I have seen students develop their skills of gratitude and contentment is through acts of service. In recent years, there has been a tremendous increase in student participation in volunteer opportunities. I rarely have to persuade or cajole students into taking part in these service-oriented activities, whether it is providing blankets and food to the homeless, tutoring children, raking leaves for the elderly, serving meals to shut-ins, making gifts for orphans, or providing school supplies to poor children in another country.

For the last eight years, I have been involved in a yearly service trip to El Progreso, Honduras. When students return home, they always report the same thing: they feel grateful for their lives. I used to think that this gratitude was the result of comparing their lives of plenty with the evident scarcity among the people we served. I have become convinced that this is not where their sense of gratitude originates. They are affected because they have just spent several days with people who live in challenging circumstances, with few comforts or luxuries, but are full of life, gratitude and contentment.

For those who see it for the first time, it is stunning. It challenges their assumption that happiness is rooted in the number of comforts they possess or the good circumstances they live in. The relationships they build among those who have much less than they do, tell them, in no uncertain terms, that happiness is a state of mind, and not simply the result of having more stuff or an easy life.

Choosing to participate in volunteer projects will take some planning but it will be worth it. Don't let your involvement with service cease after you are out of college. You might check with local civic groups, churches or even your college for opportunities to stay involved.

The following websites that can help you find volunteer projects in your area and abroad.

Volunteer abroad – www.ceciskids.org, www.volunteerhq.org, www.crossculturalsolutions.org.

Volunteer at home - www.homelessshelterdirectory.org, www.habitat.org.

The Discipline of Service

After some research, make a list of five possible service opportunities in your area. Then locate area agencies or organizations that facilitate these projects. Make a plan to include acts of service in your monthly calendar.

1. Serve in a soup kitchen if you are in a city.

2. Volunteer in a neighborhood retirement community.

3. Help build a home with Habitat for Humanity.

4. Participate in a local fund raising activity.

The discipline of gratitude will improve your life now, but more importantly, it will allow you to enjoy all the victories and successes coming toward you in the future. It will also help you face many of the discouragements and hindrances that inevitably come along as well. In this "Summer" section, I have described a few of the challenges and potential setbacks in discovering and living the life you desire. Practicing gratitude can provide the nourishment and refreshment we need for the many hot and dry moments ahead.

Becoming a grateful person is not something you are born with. It may be easier for those who have good models or who have practiced more over the years. But, it is something we can all learn to do. It is a skill we must continually practice if we hope to experience joy, happiness, and satisfaction in our progress toward living our dreams.

REMEMBER

❖ Pursuing your dreams is not selfishness. It is stewardship.

❖ Gratitude is a state of mind that can prevent you from missing out on the amazing reality of being alive right now in this moment of history.

❖ When we feel lucky or fortunate we are experiencing the emotion of gratitude.

❖ Happiness is gratefulness.

❖ Gratitude is a mentality that refuses to believe that the bad circumstances are the whole story.

❖ Your ability to be amazed at the world, maintain gratitude in the face of difficulty, see more than just misfortune, will have a direct correlation with your ability to enjoy reaching your goals.

FALL
EVALUATION AND RENEWAL

Fall may be the most surprising season of all. For many, it is their favorite time of year, and quite possibly it is the unexpected wonder that makes the season so enjoyable. Who would guess that a hot, dry, or sticky summer could give way to the beautiful leaf colors, bright blue skies, and the joyful celebrations of harvest?

At least where I live in Virginia, fall is festival time–celebrating the yield of apples, blueberries, pumpkins and much more. Artisans show up from across the state to sell their crafts, jewelry or paintings, displaying the results of their hard work and patience. Fall harvest festivals take place all over the world.

It is interesting to me that the Jewish New Year occurs in the fall. The festival of Rosh Hashanah, known as the day of Remembrance, Judgment and Renewal, falls between September 5 and October 5. The word judgment is sometimes defined as punishment, but this is a very narrow interpretation. Judgment, as understood in the festival of Rosh Hashanah, is the act of "taking stock." We ask, "How am I doing in the pursuit of my life goals, and where am I going from here?" The festival of the New Year is also known as the Feast of Trumpets. The blowing of the Shofar, an ancient horn, was used for many ceremonial purposes in the history of Israel. Rosh Hashanah is a call to take an honest look at your progress, correct your mistakes, and set your sights on the year to come.

Our metaphorical year is coming to an end and in Chapter Eleven we will discuss an important perspective on the topic of evaluation and judgment. You need not fear honest assessment or correction because your identity and worth are not up for negotiation. You are appraising your direction, actions and results, not your value. This distinction determines the difference between truly discovering your dreams or just spinning your wheels. Success in reaching your goals and finding your heart's desire depends to a great degree on embracing this crucial outlook on your human worth.

In our final chapter, we will look forward to what might come next for you. The New Year is about evaluating past action, but also about facing the future with hope. How can you take what you have learned, and build upon it in the months and years to come? For your vision to remain vital and inspiring, you must continue to refresh your intentions and targets. On any long journey we must remember to take a moment to consult our compass, examine the map, and then finally, reaffirm our direction for the road ahead.

CHAPTER ELEVEN

EMBRACE YOUR VALUE

When you understand your value and
worth as inherent and non-negotiable, your
actions become expressions of individuality
and creativity and not efforts to gain some
level of importance as a human being.

We live in a competitive world. As young children, our free and unbridled performances begin as the natural overflow of energy, exuberance, and enthusiasm. Soon we start to notice that the better performers are getting more attention, longer applauses, and louder praise. Before long, we are defining ourselves by our accomplishments, achievements, and successes. This chapter is not an effort to pass judgment on this competitive reality or to prescribe ways to alter it, but rather, a presentation of other factors that deserve thoughtful consideration on the topic of your identity as a person.

Your value is connected to all we have been saying about discovering and living your dreams. I am not referring to "your values," as in those beliefs and ideals that are most significant to you. We have already spent a considerable amount of time describing how your values influence your dreams and life plans. Think of the word "value" as that which makes you valuable as a person. *Values* describe what is important to you, but *value* is what makes you important.

Where does our sense of value or significance come from? How does anyone develop feelings of personal worth and dignity? Behind our desires to live our dreams and accomplish our goals is the hope that these actions and efforts will result in feelings of well-being and happiness. We are motivated by the desire to live a meaningful and fulfilling life. In fact, the question about what you want in life could be rephrased as "what do you believe will make your life feel gratifying and full?" Your answers to the above questions about value, will determine whether or not this dreaming and planning effort will in fact result in the desired outcome, no matter what you accomplish or achieve.

We have a choice to make when it comes to our value and worth. Either we work to get it, or we work to embrace it. And these are two different internal approaches to discovering your value. You either have potential value, determined by your accomplishments, or you have inherent value based upon your birthright. It is either a possibility to be earned, or it is a non-negotiable reality to be recognized and received.

Feeling valuable and worthwhile takes effort either way. You can work hard to *become* successful enough to feel acceptable, significant, and worthwhile, or you can work hard to *believe* that you are already acceptable, significant, and worthwhile, apart from your achievements. It is a vital distinction and one you must understand if you want this process of discovering and living your dreams to work. Because what good is it if you achieve great things but still feel empty and lost? Success is finding the fulfillment you are looking for, not just reaching your goals.

The World of Earned Value

At some point, early in life, we come to believe that we will feel valuable and worthwhile by excelling at some activity or skill. For example, if I can become good at playing the piano, or a sport, or get good grades in school, I will feel valuable and important.

But we don't start out thinking this way. One of the reasons we see such freedom and enthusiasm in young children is because they do not live with this internal demand for performance. Their clear sense of inherent value results in expressions of creativity, energy, and fun. But quickly, this sense of embraced and enjoyed value is challenged by the world of comparison and competition. They may notice that people seem more interested in them when they do something really good, brave, or impressive. They begin to observe that some are better than others at certain things and get more attention for their excellence.

It is here that the challenge to our value begins. Maybe we aren't as valuable as we originally thought and maybe we need to work a little harder for it. We begin to lose our grip on some of that inherent value as we move into the world of performance and success. Along with that loss comes the slipping away of our feelings of well-being, confidence and contentment. We wonder if maybe we need to find an area where we can excel and get more attention for our efforts and accomplishments.

We imagine if we perform well enough maybe we will regain that earlier sense of significance. Because our feelings of well-being were challenged by the world of achievement, we assume that the way to regain our sense of value and significance is to join in and excel. We are unskilled, both personally and socially, at returning to those feelings of inherent value that provided such freedom and creativity in the beginning. We didn't have to work to feel that way so we're unsure about what to do in order to feel that way again.

Efforts at Self Esteem
Attentive parents recognize this dilemma and want their children to feel good about themselves. In an effort to build a healthy sense of self in their children, parents will sometimes counteract the world of comparison by praising their children as much as possible; hoping that their admiration will translate into confidence and security. Praise is helpful for a time, but as children grow up, the praise of parents and relatives cannot stem the tide of comparison and condemnation coming from everywhere else.

Sometimes parents will agree together to try and delay the harshness of competition when their children are young. They may give blue ribbons to all participants, or not keep score at younger children's sporting events. Unfortunately for these parents, even at a very young age children know how to count. Competition seeps into their pores from every direction and keeping it out is like holding back a tidal wave with sand bags. Other parents will try to encourage their children to shine in at least one area or talent, hoping that their ability or skill in this one endeavor will help them feel special and important.

These measures are well intentioned and commendable, but none are ultimately able to counteract the inevitable world of reward and punishment that waits outside those early years of protection. We all eventually lose out to the world of "not good enough" and "just try a little harder."

In contrast to this, when your value and worth are understood as inherent and non-negotiable, your actions can become expressions of individuality and creativity, rather than efforts to gain some level of importance as a human being. We cannot overcome the negative messages coming from the world of comparison and competition by performing better or by pretending it doesn't exist.

Success in achieving a sense of value is possible only if we're willing to engage on a different playing field. The reason the performance battle is impossible to win is because there will always be someone else who is better than you and who gets more praise than you do. Plus, you will always know that you could do a little bit better or achieve a little more. If your value is based upon performance, then your performances will never be quite good enough, even if you are really good.

You won't be quite smart enough, talented enough, brave enough, pretty enough, rich enough, powerful enough, or anything enough. I once asked a group of students; "if you need to be smart in order to feel valuable, how smart do you need to be?" Answer: "Just a little bit smarter." If you need to be pretty in order to feel attractive, how pretty do you need to be? "Just a little prettier." You may have a superior talent, or be a stunning beauty, but there will always be someone or something that undermines your confidence.

Facing the Competition and Comparison

In this exercise, I want you to face the world of comparison you are living in right now. Make a list of qualities or skills you believe would help you feel better about yourself. Keep writing until you have filled up at least one page. Be very specific. Work on this list for a week. Once you are finished take it outside and light it on fire.

1. If I weighed less or had more muscle definition.

2. If I was smarter or had a degree from a good school.

3. If I had more money.

4. If I was better looking.

So how does one reconnect with that feeling of freedom, creativity and play we possessed as children before we were thrust into the world of conditional value and worth? How can you balance conditional value and worth with an ongoing reminder that this isn't the only world that exists?

The World of Unconditional Value

Since the *earned value* system is always open for reevaluation and revision, and built around competition and comparison, it can never be secure. In this system we draw conclusions about ourselves based upon a structure of rewards and punishments. If we do well, we feel valuable, if not, we feel worthless.

Unconditional value says that our worth is rooted in our humanity and is not open for negotiation or debate. This system stands in direct opposition to the earned system. This is the way we felt about ourselves as young children when our sense of well-being and value were enjoyed by virtue of being born. The problem with maintaining the realities and results of this belief system is that we must do so in the face of the other world which often shouts our defectiveness and inadequacy. From a very young age, we experienced the results of comparison and competition both in the classroom as well as the playground.

We need a strategy for engaging in this battle. We can't simply try really hard to feel good about ourselves when the world of "try-a-little-harder" is all around us. Sometimes the conclusions we make concerning our dignity and worth have been ingrained from an early age.

It will help to recognize that each one of us participates in the *earned value* world. There is no way of removing ourselves from an environment that will assign worth and value in response to our talents, accomplishments, and skills. As we move toward our dreams and goals, we need to remind ourselves daily that no matter what I achieve or attain, it won't make me feel more worthwhile or significant. We must fight against the temptation to try and add to our sense of importance through achievements.

Benefits of Unconditional Value

The famous psychologist Carl Rogers called it "unconditional positive regard" and he developed a therapeutic model based upon it. The client is respected, and treated as a person, rather than as an object to be manipulated, fixed, or directed. He once wrote, "The curious paradox is that when I accept myself just as I am, then I can change."[1] Later in life, his belief in the dignity, worth, and capability of all people led to his interest and involvement in the conflict in Ireland between Catholics and Protestants. He also worked to help end apartheid in South Africa.[2] Here is a list of several benefits that come from recognizing our value as non-negotiable and settled.

First benefit - You can develop a more accurate picture about what you really want. If the only reason you want something is because it will make you feel better about yourself, then it may not be a true desire at all. A true passion is something that exists even if no one is looking, praising, or noticing. Being praised is a nice outcome for a job well done, but a true passion flows from within, before it's evaluated by others. If you love to sing, then you enjoy doing it even if no one is tuning in. An authentic desire and interest will be fulfilling and enjoyable because it is a true expression of your uniqueness and creativity, but your sense of value and worth remains unchanged.

Second Benefit - Embracing unconditional value creates a more relaxed honesty about your abilities and talents. Those who object to the concept of unconditional value claim that it removes the basis for evaluation between good and bad. They conclude it makes people sloppy or lazy, but it does just the opposite. It makes us freer to talk about good musicians, talented baseball players, skillful mathematicians or artistic de-signers. It gives us greater freedom to acknowledge that there will always be someone who performs at a higher level than us and others at a lower level, and that fact doesn't make me feel better than or worse than anyone else.

You become more agreeable to learn from people more skilled than you and more willing to help those who may need your help. You actually enjoy the results of success because the ef-fort flows from fullness and true passion.

Third Benefit- You will be less panicked about making mistakes. As mentioned before, your mistakes are not a commentary on your worth as a human being but rather an aspect of the learn-ing process. Therefore, you will feel freer to take chances and more willing to learn from your failures. There is no need to

pretend that you are better than you are. You will be more willing to try something new even if you are unskilled at it at first.
You can be open to learn and not afraid of needing improvement. When your value is no longer at stake, you can explore
with great freedom and enthusiasm.

What is true in life is that sometimes we succeed and other
times we fail. But the only way we can be free to acknowledge
and accept this reality is when our worth as human beings is
not tied to always succeeding. We become extremely sensitive
about making mistakes, having weaknesses, or failing, when we
are only playing on the performance field.

*Fourth Benefit - Unconditional value generates a patient ap-
proach to your dreams and life goals.* When you are trying to
get value through success or achievement you become more
desperate and frantic about reaching your objectives. Despera-
tion and panic will create short bursts of energy and productivity, but usually these periods are extremely hectic, stressful
and short lived. For the most part, discovering your dreams
and direction is a life-long pursuit and involves a process that
takes patience, persistence and strong resolve. Embracing your
unconditional value will give you a greater chance to enjoy the
journey.

*Fifth Benefit – By embracing your unconditional value, you
become better equipped to discover community and togeth-
erness.* No longer needing to be the "best" or the "only," you
can freely connect with others who have like-minded interests.
You can help others who may be seeking a similar outlet for
their desires and dreams. Living your dream will become less
lonely and more shared. Anyone who wants to express their
interests in a particular way or in a specific arena is welcomed
and encouraged to do so. You will feel free to serve and help

others because you are less fearful about not being noticed, acknowledged or rewarded. You will discover the joy in living authentically from your true interests and desires, and not simply to get enough praise.

Sixth Benefit – You will have more fun in pursuing your dream when your value is not connected to your successes. It is ironic sometimes that the most miserable people seem to be those trying so desperately to find happiness through success. When your sense of well-being is rooted in the performance game, your satisfaction will be temporary at best. But lasting and peaceful enjoyment is possible when your value is not dependent on your achievements. You will be free to enjoy your efforts and progress when you are working from a solid and secure sense of worth.

Strategy for Embracing Your Value
So here is the question. What do you do regularly that reminds you that you're valuable, special, worthwhile and significant just because you are a human being and simply because you were born?

One of my professors in graduate school once told our class that he had never met a secure person. Everyone is insecure, he claimed. I thought that was a very bold statement at the time but over the years I've come to agree with him. When he made that statement in a large lecture class, you could almost hear the collective sigh of relief because the only thing more difficult than feeling insecure is the notion that you're the only one who feels that way.

Having a strategy to deal with your sense of value is as important as having a plan to live your dreams. Just as your dreams and plans develop throughout your lifetime, so will your ability to embrace your inherent value and worth. No one becomes an expert at these things. A strategy for developing a solid and sustainable sense of self is a vital foundation for everything you would like to accomplish through the many stages of your life.

Self-improvement is not a strategy for embracing your value or increasing your self-esteem. It is a strategy for self-improvement, period. The value question is about who you are apart from what you do. Here are a few ideas on how to do it.

First Strategy - Celebrate your birthday. Every year celebrate your birthday in a way that pays attention to the wonder of your existence and the gift of being alive. Invite your friends to celebrate with you but don't wait for them to take action on your behalf. Your birthday is truly the most important event in the world for you. Without it, you don't exist. So celebrate. Plan it and make it happen. This is at the root of your value. You did not show up an empty slate devoid of value. Rather, all the value that you now have was with you on the day you were born. Nothing you have done since that day has added even a small fraction to the value and worth present at your birth. This is a very important realization that you will need to remind yourself time and time again.

Second Strategy - Research the meaning of your name. A mentor of mine once said that it is far more important *"that"* you are named than *"what"* you are named. By researching your name, understanding its meaning and its origin, you can remember and reflect on the significance of being personally and uniquely named. One day, you entered the world and were given a personal name chosen especially for you. Eugene Peterson writes:

> *At our birth we are named, not numbered. The name is that part of speech by which we are recognized as a*

person. We are not classified as a species of animal. We are not labeled as a compound of chemicals. We are not assessed for our economic potential and given a cash value. We are named.[3]

You didn't earn a name after you proved yourself worthy of being a part of the human race. You were given a personal name at birth and it cannot be taken away from you. It wasn't a reward for being really good at something or becoming a great success, but simply because you were welcomed into the world as a person. Being named is the most important personal thing about you. Throughout your life you will receive titles, rewards, trophies, acknowledgements but nothing will ever be more significant than your personal name. It is one of the reasons we don't like it when people call us by the wrong name or why it feels so good when someone we recently met remembers it. When our names are remembered, we feel acknowledged; not for what we have done, but for who we are. So honor your name, even if you don't especially like it. It was given to you early and declares a basic foundational reality about your personal value and uniqueness in the world.

Third Strategy - Discover and collect identity stories that tell you the truth about who you are. Culture has always shaped ideas about life from the stories that are remembered and passed on to successive generations. I'm not sure we in the west are very skilled at remembering and retelling value stories. Maybe it has been drilled out of us by advertisers who sell us products based upon a "not good enough" message. Some of these value stories are ancient and more universal in scope; often preserved in our many religious traditions. Others are more contemporary and specific to a particular local culture or region.

People use religious stories for many different reasons, some good and others less so. Religious stories can create tremendous motivation and energy for living our lives to the fullest and can help create communities that ritualize and memorialize these values for each other. Some people believe that religion's primary purpose is telling us how to live a good life or what it means to be moral. Although this is an important discussion in society, it is not the most important function for our religious traditions. As human beings, understanding our identity and unconditional value is a critical foundation to making any decisions about how to live. We need a way to stay focused on our non-negotiable significance as we set out to express our unique contribution in the world.

Every religion has a story about inherent value. Sometimes these identity stories are overshadowed by other purposes such as behavioral reform, political action or ideological support. How we behave as individuals or as a society are important questions we all must answer, and religion is often pulled into the conversation to justify and defend one opinion or another.

The powerful stories of faith that express our unconditional value are occasionally hijacked by those trying to persuade us or even manipulate us to behave a certain way or join their political cause. It can be confusing when the same religious stories are frequently interpreted differently by those trying to use them to propagate opposite positions.

So while we argue about the best way to live as individuals or as a society, who is helping us stay focused on what it means to be a valued, worthwhile human being? While some stories are used as a way to get recruits for their cause or project, I suggest we find stories that can be used to help fight against the "trying-to-be-good-enough" world of performance, comparison and competition.

Two Lost Sons

One such identity story is called "The Prodigal Son."[4] It is a story about a father and his two sons. One day, the younger son decides that he wants to leave home, so he asks his father for an early draw on his inheritance and runs off to a distant country. There, the story says that he squanders his inheritance on irresponsible living and bad choices. When the money and his friends disappear, he ends up feeding pigs on a farm without enough money to even feed himself.

One day it occurs to him that even the servants in his father's house have at least three meals a day. So he decides to return home, admit that he no longer deserves to be called a son, and ask to be given a job as one of his father's hired hands. After the long journey home, the father sees him coming from a distance and runs to him in relief and overwhelming happiness, having thought that his son was dead. To the younger son's surprise, his father doesn't pay attention to his prepared speech or planned remorse, but rather calls for new clothes, a new ring, and a big party to welcome his son home.

In the meantime, the older son, who always tried to do the right thing, stays away in frustration because of the way his younger brother was being welcomed back. He was confused. Why is his brother getting such good treatment when he acted so badly? The father goes out to his older, obedient son to convince him that his affection toward him is the same as for his younger brother. The older son complains that what the father was doing wasn't fair. The younger son didn't deserve to be treated with this much excitement and enthusiasm. He argues that he'd been obedient his whole life and this "miserable son of yours" has done nothing but squander his life. Why does he deserve a party?

Both sons were lost in performance-based value. Both believed that their identity and worth were related to their ability to achieve. The younger one tried to deal with this pressure by rebelling against it, while the older one tried harder and harder to be perfect. The younger son couldn't be bad enough, and older son couldn't be good enough, to free themselves from the intense burden of earned value. Neither one was able to recognize or enjoy the value and worth that was theirs simply by being born as a cherished son in their father's house.

The younger son needed to know that the party was not given because he deserved it, while the older son needed to know that all the robes, rings and fatted calves were always his from the start. No amount of good performance and no amount of bad performance made either of them any more or less acceptable, valuable, worthwhile or loved.

The younger son seems to finally understand it when his father lavishes upon him a welcome home robe, a ring, and a fatted calf in spite of behavior that landed him in the pig sty. The older son has a chance to realize it when he sees his father's reaction to his younger brother's return. Both needed to understand and embrace that there was something true about them apart from their performances, good or bad. These two sons were accepted without strings, conditions or exceptions from the moment of their birth, and nothing could ever add to or detract from their non-negotiable value.[5]

This story has been used in a variety of ways throughout history. It has been used to tell people to avoid being bad or you'll end up in a pig sty; or if we are really sorry for our bad behavior, and willing to change our ways, we will be given another chance. Both of these interpretations would miss the central and more crucial message about value. Embracing our unconditional value is the foundational core for everything we do in life.

Find stories that deliver this message, and replay them over and over again. When you begin looking, you will see them everywhere..

A well-known speaker started off his seminar by holding up a $20.00 bill. In the room of 200, he asked, "Who would like this $20 bill?" Hands started going up. He said, "I am going to give this $20 to one of you but first, let me do this. He proceeded to crumple up the $20 dollar bill. He then asked, "Who still wants it?" Still the hands were up in the air. Well, he replied, "What if I do this?" And he dropped it on the ground. And started to grind it into the floor with his shoe. He picked it up, now crumpled and dirty. "Now, who still wants it?" Still the hands went into the air. My friends, he said, we have all learned a very valuable lesson. No matter what I did to the money, you still wanted it because it did not decrease in value. It was still worth $20. Many times in our lives, we are dropped, crumpled, and ground into the dirt by the decisions we make and the circumstances that come our way. We feel as though we are worthless. But no matter what has happened or what will happen, you will never lose your value. Dirty or clean, crumpled or finely creased, you are still priceless to those who DO LOVE you. The worth of our lives comes not in what we do or who we know, But by WHO WE ARE.

Fourth Strategy - Discover and cultivate non-competitive, supportive friendships. We need to be around people who care about us in spite of our shortcomings and failures. Sometimes these kinds of friendships take time to cultivate. Often we have known these people for a long time; they may have seen us through a variety of stages and phases in life. I love this quote by the great golfer Phil Michelson about his family, *"My family has reduced the effect of my career on my self-esteem. When I'm with them, they make me feel special regardless of how I play."*

My encouragement to you is to work hard at maintaining your longtime friendships. Don't let distance or circumstances interrupt your connections with people who can reflect your unconditional value and identity. Be brave enough to let go of relationships that do the opposite. Let go of those that make you feel unworthy, devalued or inferior. If you always have to prove yourself to someone in order to feel liked, then move on. If you can find a community of friends where maintaining each other's value and significance is more important than becoming honored and successful, then stay connected to them.

One model community that does a good job reflecting unconditional value and acceptance is Alcoholics Anonymous. One of the many reasons for the success of AA in helping people stay sober is their ability to communicate value and worth to everyone who joins the meeting regardless of their success or failure with their addiction. The secret of AA is that they treat people as special, important and wanted before they are successful in getting free from their dependency on alcohol or drugs. They know that behind all bad choices is the debilitating feeling of shame and self-rejection. Everyone needs a place where they are valued for who they are, not for what they have done or accomplished. Ultimately that message, once believed and acted upon, can provide the strength and courage to move away from unhealthy behavior.

Fifth Strategy - Become a Daymaker. One of the best books I've read recently is David Wagner's *Life as a Daymaker*. It is a description of the way David found happiness and value by trying to bring happiness and value to others in his life. He is a hairdresser by trade, but his motivation is to "make someone's day," wherever and whenever he can. He discovered that as he focused on those around him, worked in small ways to bring something extra or unexpected, the encouragement he gave to others, splashed back onto him. He says, he no longer viewed himself simply as a hairdresser. That was simply the environment for his larger and more important work of bringing gladness, gratitude and value into the lives of those he met. "If we live with the intent of being Daymakers in everything we do, we will not only change our own lives, but the lives of everyone around us."[6]

There is no better way to embrace your own value than in the practice of treating others with value and appreciation. Why not give this exercise a try. For the next thirty days, "make someone's day." Instead of random acts of kindness, do an intentional deed of compassion. You must notice, listen and be creative, but it is actually much easier than you think. Keep track of your experiences in a journal.

Become a "Daymaker" for a Month

1. Double the size of your tip the next time you eat at a restaurant.

2. Send your parents flowers thanking them for giving you life.

3. Write an email to an associate telling them you appreciate their friendship.

4. Send a card to a friend you haven't seen in a while telling them you miss them.

5. Give a bottle of water to the mailman just because he might be thirsty.

6. Next time you wash your car, wash your neighbor's car at the same time.

7. Write an appreciative note to one of your college professors.

You will be surprised by the way in which bringing value to other people can help you embrace your unconditional value and worth. By acting in this way toward others we are reminded about what makes us important and significant.

Embracing your value is the bedrock attitude for all your life goals. It will be difficult to sustain a life-long pursuit of your dreams without it. It is the foundational understanding that will strengthen your resolve, and create a peaceful, joyful mentality for the journey ahead.

REMEMBER

❖ Discovering and achieving your dreams will never cause you to feel more valuable.

❖ The only way to enjoy reaching your dreams is to believe that your value, acceptance and worth are not dependent on your success.

❖ If the only reason you want something is because it will make you feel better about yourself, then it may not be a true desire at all.

❖ Reaching for your dreams is not an effort to find your value, or to become significant, but rather a creative way to express the value and significance you already possess.

❖ Our choice: We can either work to create our own value and worth, or we can work to visualize, embrace, and express the value that is inherently ours at birth.

CHAPTER TWELVE
RENEW YOUR VISION

Twenty years from now you will be more disappointed
by the things that you didn't do than by the ones you
did do. So throw off the bowlines. Sail away from the
safe harbor. Catch the trade winds in your sails.
Explore. Dream. Discover.
Mark Twain

You are well aware by now that this process of moving from your formal education to the rest of your life will take time, effort, and patience. If this book has done nothing other than give you a few traveling tips for the road ahead, point out some of the unique challenges and opportunities before you, and lower your level of fear and anxiety about the journey, then it has done its job.

Cultural Shift
Throughout history, the greatest periods of cultural transformation occur when society experiences a breakthrough in the area

of communications. For example, six hundred years ago, the invention of the printing press drove the powerful and dramatic social transformations of the Renaissance. More recently, the rapid social changes in the late nineteenth and early twentieth centuries were the result of the invention of electricity, the telegraph, telephone, automobile, and airplane.

Now, only a hundred years later, with the invention and rapid development of computer technology, some have suggested that we may be involved in one of the most profound and widespread social transformations in the history of the world. Salman Kahn, founder of the Kahn Academy and innovative leader in education, says, "Among the world's children starting grade school this year, sixty-five percent will end up doing jobs that haven't even been invented yet."[1]

Those of you in your twenties can attest first hand to the social changes occurring in the growing-up process. The ground has shifted under your feet and the path to adulthood has become both extended and cluttered. You are like a group of travelers crossing a bridge, who suddenly begin to notice that the huge concrete pillars, metal trusses, enormous anchors and cables are starting to sway, crack, and give way. The entire bridge is looking like it may, at any moment, collapse with you on it. Doing your best to stay positive, you just keep walking forward, hoping to make it to the other side.

Everyone told you that this was the bridge that had carried millions of people to adulthood. So you jumped on and started walking forward, passing marker after marker, indicating that adulthood was just up ahead. As you graduated from college, you thought surely you would be nearing the finish line. Unfortunately, if you recently received your diploma, the "other side" isn't even in view, and the bridge designed to get you across is looking less and less reliable.

Getting Unstuck

Edwin Friedman, in *A Failure of Nerve*, has used the great maritime explorations of the sixteenth century to describe the way any organization, family, community, or country can become stuck in approaches, methods, and motivations that no longer work. At the turn of the sixteenth century, Europe became oriented to a new way of imagining the world, and the resulting new discoveries and breakthroughs were coming into conflict with old structures.[2]

The word "orientation" or "toward the Orient" comes from the way people of that time viewed the world. The focus of the entire culture was oriented toward the east. Very few, says Friedman, ever imagined that anything existed "behind them." He uses this period of world history as an extended metaphor to discuss the way cultures, countries, organizations, or families can get trapped in rigidity and fear.

When it comes to the transition into adulthood, our society is definitely stuck. It appears that most still believe that the path to a successful and fulfilling adult life passes through a college education. In fact, that is the only idea we seem to have. We are still holding on to the notion that if you do well in college, get good grades, become a student leader, and collect honors, you will find a good job that will provide the stability and permanence needed for a truly happy and gratifying life. But as we have discussed, that is clearly no longer enough.

Consequently, young people all over the country and their families, accumulate enormous debt, spend years of their lives pursuing skills they may never need, in order to get a certificate that says they put in the time and paid their dues. But many are beginning to realize that their formal education actually didn't prepare them adequately for their move into a settled adulthood, let alone land a good-paying job. Many emerging adults leave college wondering, "Where is the life that was promised when I signed up?" Some of you would like a refund. If you want to watch an entertaining and revealing parody of the current job/college scenario, watch the video at www.theonion.com/video/company-immediately-calls-job-applicant-upon-seein,31670/.

Personally I loved school, and continued my formal education for a long time. School has its place in society for jobs that require certificates or specialized skills. But when it comes to creating an adult life, a life of your own choosing that fits with your dreams and desires, much more is needed. Things may change someday, but for now, you must take charge of your own education and develop the necessary skills to move your life forward. You cannot wait for someone in authority to come along, take you by the hand, and lead you to the promised land of adulthood. Hopefully, colleges and universities will begin to realize that they cannot continue to do their job of educating the next generation of adults in the same old ways and expect to not eventually get fired—because it isn't working for most.

Explore and Experiment
As you begin to explore the many possibilities before you, take appropriate risks, and develop strategies for a hopeful future, you will make some mistakes along the way. But as I have said often, don't let that risk stop you from pursuing your dreams and planning your future. In a social environment like ours, it is the only way forward.

In discussing the transformative changes in world perceptions, Friedman points out that mistakes or errors took on a different and far less significant role when the quest was driven by adventure and possibility, rather than safety and security. He says,

> To say that mistakes are unimportant may overstate the case somewhat; yet Europe's reorientation process clearly demonstrates that even though huge errors were made along the way, some lasting for more than a century, they turned out to be a small price to pay for getting the ships out of the harbor.[3]

Explorers such as Cartier, Verrazzano, Magellan, da Gama, and Columbus were able to do what they did because there was something larger and more significant at stake than simply being accurate all of the time. They developed a much higher tolerance for mistakes in light of the new discoveries now within their imaginative vision.

Some scholars have claimed that the Age of Discovery was the result of the intellectual and economic advances occurring at that time. In other words, they say that the Renaissance gave birth to exploration. But Friedman suggests that it may have been the other way around. He believes that the overwhelming surge in intellectual creativity found in the Renaissance may in fact have been motivated by the expanding imagination of the early navigators and their supporters, particularly due to the discovery of a new continent. As explorers literally threw caution to the wind when the possibility of a new world was discovered, and as they began to realize the transforming power and world-changing magnitude of what they were seeing and experiencing, their enthusiasm and energy spread to an entire population.

As today's emerging adults, you must view yourselves as explorers who are braving the high seas, searching for new routes and new lands, rather than merely city dwellers taking over your parents' businesses. This is much bigger than simply finding a new road to a well-paying job. The world is changing and we can hardly imagine what the new one will look like in connection with the growing-up process.

At some point in the future, people may read about this period of history as the "Age of Discovery" in the adult development process. Each of you, as emerging adults, are a part of this reorientation as you discover and create new ways to deal with the challenges and opportunities available in our modern society.

Change is the New Normal

One thing seems clear; the world of the mass market is beginning to weaken. Fewer and fewer people are watching the same TV shows, going to the same movies, or listening to the same music. We are seeing the rapid rise of smaller tribes and clans who possess their own perspectives, interests, and appetites. The day of the cookie-cutter consumer is losing steam, and the world of individual tastes, ambitions, motivations, and inspirations is gaining ground.

Soon, young people will begin to realize that the process of education is not the same for everyone. We will begin to respect and value other ways to become prepared for the life we envision. For too long, we have resigned ourselves to the educational experts to tell us what we need to know and how we need to think in order to be successful and prepared. And although their advice is helpful, it is simply no longer sufficient. That advice also does not take into account the many thousands of people in our society for whom the school process and method does not work. Often, they are left feeling either like second class citizens or not as smart as those who succeed in college.

As emerging adults, you will need something more, because you are leaving college, degree in hand, without a clue about the next steps. Older adults must not close their ears to the reality of what is happening in society and pretend all will be well for this generation of emerging adults if they just stay the course. Today's graduates must discover new roads to an adult life because the old one is breaking down. The good news is; you are not alone.

What I've written here is just a beginning for emerging adults who are in this developmental "age of discovery." You are the Magellans, the Cartiers, and the da Gamas for the generations to follow. You will be a part of the answer as you construct new roads and reliable pathways to adulthood. The old bridge will not survive, as many of you can attest, and yet your drive to get to the other side remains strong, determined, and hopeful.

All of the ideas and skills we have discussed in this book are centered around you taking charge of your future. If you have been doing the work this past year then you are probably well on your way to creating the life you want. Because you are among the first generation to chart these waters, like the early explorers, you will make a few mistakes. Don't worry, just keep moving forward; make corrections when necessary and renew your vision often.

Bravery and Courage

Don't get discouraged if other people question your objectives or strategy. Friedman points out that it was nearly two hundred years before people of Europe gave up their notion of a flat Earth, even after the explorers returned with evidence of lands across the sea.

Questioning and challenging traditional approaches to the process of growth and development takes bravery and courage. But the more people who take on this challenge, and demonstrate that other routes to adulthood exist, the easier it will be for the next generation of emerging adults to follow.

Be patient as you continue to work through the skills and exercises in this book. It should be clear by now that these skills are not just about getting a job or figuring out how to make money. You do not need this book to learn how to do that. There are plenty of books on writing résumés, interviewing successfully, locating want ads, etc. I have been talking about discovering and living your dream in all areas of your life.

The way forward is more personal and individual than in the past. You cannot be squeezed into a container of someone else's making. You will be building your own container, shaped according to your interests, passions, and abilities. It is both scary and exciting work. This is why the next steps will not be mine to design for you. They will be yours to discover, plan, and initiate for yourself.

It will be a specific curriculum for just one student—you. The only fitting end to this book is the ending you write for yourself. This ending becomes the beginning of the next chapter of your life. To quote Shakespeare from his play *The Tempest*: "What is past is prologue." Below you will see a chart for the next six months to get you started. You must decide what needs to happen in those months and what topics will serve as the guiding focus for you as you continue to make your way toward the life you desire.

Maybe through the course of this past year you noticed some additional work that was needed in one or more of the areas. You could begin there. Or maybe there was an important topic that you feel was left out altogether. Use your imagination and keep moving.

You need six categories for the next six months. You will define the objective, decide on the needed research, and figure out what exercises might be necessary in order to accomplish your goals. I will be interested in seeing your work and will always be available to you for feedback or suggestions. So get to work. You've got the rest of your life waiting to be discovered and lived.

I invite you to join me at www.yourfifthyear.com for further help and resources. This is not an easy task as most of you realize by now. The website will allow you to receive further coaching or community support for the days and months ahead. Don't put it off. The road before you is not a short one, but it promises to be an amazing journey as you continue to discover your dreams and learn how to make them real day by day throughout the rest of your life.

> *"There is something you must always remember, you are braver than you believe, stronger than you seem, and smarter than you think."*
> — *Christopher Robin to Winnie the Pooh*

Month One_____

_____
_____
_____
_____
_____
_____
_____
_____

Month Two_____

_____
_____
_____
_____
_____
_____
_____

Month Three_____

_____
_____
_____
_____
_____
_____
_____

Month Four_____

_____
_____
_____
_____
_____
_____
_____
_____

Month Five_____

_____
_____
_____
_____
_____
_____
_____
_____

Month Six_____

_____
_____
_____
_____
_____
_____
_____
_____

ACKNOWLEDGEMENTS

I couldn't have finished this book without the constant encouragement (and occasional prodding) from my family and friends. I have an amazing gift for procrastination and postponement. It's uncanny how many things on my to-do list become urgent the moment I sit down to write.

Thank you to all the students, present and former, who took the time to read early versions of the manuscript and make very helpful suggestions and additions. Thanks Loy, Lucy, Christine, Ainsley, Daniel, Sarah, Steph, Trevor, Nicole, Rachel, Fran, Ellen, Ashley, Alexi, Lightening, Dooley, Chelsea, and many others. You did your best to help me stay current with metaphors, illustrations and phrases that resonate best with the twenty-something life experience. Anything that slipped by your corrective net is totally on me.

Thank you to my daughter Amy, a writer by training and profession, who helped me immensely with organization, ideas, flow, grammar and much more. Thanks also to the rest of my family; Dorie and Shelley, and their husbands Kelvin and Wyatt, and our son Matt, who have amazed me in their own successful journeys into adulthood. You've always listened to my ideas, engaged with me in conversation, and shared your helpful perspectives and thoughts no matter what the topic. And a special thanks to our new granddaughter Harper and grandson Ethan, who motivated me to think about what becoming adult might mean for them in the future.

Thanks to my good friend Shin, who stayed at our house one weekend, spending hours going through the material with me, discussing ideas and providing helpful comments and suggestions. You are a good friend and your life, a constant inspiration. I still remember that morning in Tela, Honduras when we each decided to begin writing. Our early morning writing sessions, you in Honduras and me in Virginia is what got me started. Thank you also for your kind and thoughtful foreword.

Thank you to Marlene, who has been my administrative assistant for the past eleven years and who well knows how lost I'd be without her support, regular reminders, and enforced deadlines. I was able to write worry free because of your conscientious organizing ability and your seemingly effortless capacity to keep our campus program running smoothly and efficiently.

Finally, I want to thank my wife Sue who kept me going every time I became frustrated and wanted to quit. You'd patiently listen to me whine and complain when I became stuck, and talk with me about what I really wanted, which, of course, got me back to writing. But more than that, you truly believed that I could do it. You believed that I could get my ideas down on paper and make them understandable. You read and re-read my words again and again to help me clarify, rearrange, and rewrite, in order to say it as plainly and directly as possible. Any remaining mistakes or redundancy are most likely places where I refused to listen. Thank you Sue, not only for your help with the book, but for your friendship and love for over thirty-five years of marriage. That is a long time, and we're still having fun. I dedicate this book to you.

NOTES

Introduction

1. *Field of Dreams*. Dir. Phil Alden Robinson. Universal Pictures, 1989. Film.

Chapter 1 – Face a New Reality

1. Jeffrey Jensen Arnett, *Emerging Adulthood: The Winding Road from Late Teens through the Twenties* (New York: Oxford University Press, 2004).
2. Victor Turner, *Ritual Process: Structure and Anti-Structure* (New York: Aldine, 1995).
3. www.youtube.com/watch?v=ap-22FjgoE4.
4. www.theatlantic.com.
5. Eric Chester, *Getting Them to Give a Damn* (Fort Lauderdale: Kaplan Publishing, 2005), 12.

Chapter 2 – Find Your Rhythm

1. *The Truman Show*. Dir. Peter Weir. Paramount Pictures, 1998. Film.

2. Journal of Applied Social Psychology Volume 39, Issue 12, pages 2787–2797, December 2009.
3. Gretchen Rubin, *The Happiness Project.* (New York: Haper-Collins, 2009), 27.
4. Hyrum W. Smith, *The 10 Natural Laws of Successful Time and Life Management.* (New York: Warner books, 1994), 98.
5. Anne Lamont, *Bird by Bird.* (New York: Anchor Books,1994), 19.

Chapter 3 – Do Your Jobs

1. www.psychologytoday.com/blog/brain-candy/201208/make-your-bed-change-your-life.
2. Theologian and author Frederick Buechner, speaking about vocation, put it this way: "The place God calls you to is the place where your deep gladness and the world's deep hunger meet." Frederick Buechner, *Wishful Thinking: A Theological ABC.* (New York: Harper and Row, 1973), 95.
3. Seth Godin, *Linchpin* (New York: Portfolio/Penguin, 2010), 5.
4. See the article in Forbes about 55% unemployment among 2011 Law School Graduates and nearly 100 thousand dollars of school debt. www.forbes.com/sites/jmaureen-henderson/2012/06/26/why-attending-law-school-is-the-worst-career-decision-youll-ever-make.
5. Seth Godin, "Beyond Showing Up," *Seth Godin* (blog), January 28, 2013, www.sethgodin.typepad.com/seths_blog/2013/01/beyond-showing-up.
6. Matthew Crawford, *Shop Class as Soulcraft.* (New York: Penquin, 2009).
7. Joe Lamacchia, *Blue Collar & Proud Of It: The All-in-One Resource for Finding Freedom, Financial Success, and Security Outside the Cubicle.* (Deerfield Beach, FL, Health Communications, 2009).

Chapter 4 – Explore Your Dreams - Make a Plan

1. Joseph K. Vetter, Reader's Digest, July, 2005.
2. Gretchen Rubin, *The Happiness Project*. (New York: Haper-Collins, 2009).
3. Gretchen Rubin, (September, 2013). Are You Adrift? *Good Housekeeping*. 105.
4. Parker Palmer, *Let Your Life Speak*. (San Francisco: Jossey-Bass, 2000), 3.
5. Tim Ferrris, *The 4-Hour Work Week*. (New York: Crown, 2007), 58.
6. Julien Smith, *The Flinch* (The Domino Project, 2011), E-book, loc. 56.
7. Chip Heath and Dan Heath, *Decisive*. (New York: Crown, 2013), Loc. 755.
8. Leonard Schlesinger and Charles Kiefer, *Just Start: Take Action, Embrace Uncertainty, Create the Future*. (Boston: Harvard Business School Publishing, 2012), 7.
9. www.tuebingen.mpg.de/en/news-press/press-releases/detail/walking-in-circles.
10. Malcolm Gladwell, *Outliers* (New York: Back Bay Books, 2011), 38.
11. Ibid., 40.

Chapter 5 – Locate Your Resources

1. Katharine M. Rogers, Creator of Oz: *A Biography*. (New York, St. Martin's Press, 2002), 49.
2. Ibid., 89.
3. Laura Ingles, (2013, March 12-18). A Horse of a Different Color: Equine Message Therapist Combines Two Passions. *The C-Ville Weekly*. 25.
4. Derek Sivers, *Anything You Want*. (Irvington: Do You Zoom, 2011).

5. Graelyn Brashear, (2012, March 12-18) Weighing Words: An Unlikely Path to Life at a Newspaper. *The C-Ville Weekly.* 27.
6. Scott Peck, *The Road Less Traveled.* (New York, Touchstone, 1978), 1.

Chapter 6 – Take Your Chances

1. Carl Jung, *Memories, Dreams and Reflections.* (New York: Random House, 1961).
2. John Taylor Gatto, *Weapons of Mass Instruction* (Gabriola Island: New Society Publishers, 2009), *xi.*
3. www.news.stanford.edu/news/2005/june15/jobs-061505.
4. John Maxwell, *Failing Forward.* (Thomas Nelson: Nashville, 2000), 21.
5. Julien Smith, *The Flinch,* location 71.
6. Robert D. Smith, *20,000 Days and Counting.* (Thomas Neslon: Nashville, 2012), 75.
7. Ibid., 76.
8. www.rejectiontherapy.com.
9. He details his experience on his blog: www.entresting.com/blog/100-days-of-rejection-therapy.
10. www.entresting.com/blog/2012/12/25/the-need-for-rejection.
11. www.entresting.com/blog/2012/12/04/day-18-give-weather-forecast-on-live-tv.

Chapter 7 – Battle Discouragement

1. Leon Gutterman, editor. (1956, August) Jonas E. Salk, Medical Researcher. *Wisdom Magazine*, 6.
2. Ibid.
3. Tom Paulson, (2004, April 25) At the Salk family table, a long conquest is begun. *Seattle Post-Intelligencer.* 1.

4. Seth Godin, "Quieting the Lizard Brain," *Seth Godin* (blog), January 28, 2010, http://sethgodin.typepad.com/seths_blog/2010/01/quieting-the-lizard-brain.

5. Remo Jacuzzi, *Spirit, Wind & Water,* (New York: Welcome Rain Publishers, 2007), 63.

Chapter 8 – Practice Solitude

1. www.paulocoelhoblog.com/2013/03/29/solitude-is-not-the-absence-of-love.

2. John Jantsch, "The Business Case for Solitude," *Duct Tape Marketing* (blog), July 25, 2011, http://www.ducttapemarketing.com/blog/2011/07/25/the-business-case-for-solitude.

3. Shel Silverstein, *The Missing Piece Meets the Big O* (New York: Harper & Row, 1981).

Chapter 9 – Confront Fear

1. Owen Chase, Thomas Cahill, *Shipwreck of the Whaleship Essex.* (New York: The Lyons Press, 1999), 34.

2. Ibid., xxiv.

3. Barrett Seaman, *Binge.* (New Jersey: John Wiley and Sons), 1ff.

4. Joseph LeDoux, "Searching the Brain for the Roots of Fear," *Opinionator* (blog), *New York Times,* January 22, 2012, http://opinionator.blogs.nytimes.com/2012/01/22/anatomy-of-fear.

5. Ibid.

Chapter 10 – Exercise Gratitude

1. Quoted by Tim Ferris, *The 4-Hour Work Week, 306.*

2. *Joe Versus the Volcano,* Dir. John Patrick Shanley, Warner Bros., 1990. Film.

3. Michael J. Fox, *Lucky Man*. (New York: Hyperion, 2002).
4. Muir, John (1901). *Our National Parks*. (Boston: Houghton Mifflin), 43.

Chapter 11- Embrace Your Value

1. Carl Rogers, *On Becoming a Person*. (New York: Houghton Mifflin Harcourt, 1961) 10.
2. www.nndb.com/people/910/000164418.
3. Eugene Peterson, *Run with the Horses* (Madison, WI: Intervarsity Press, 1983), 25.
4. The Prodigal Son can be read in the Gospel of Luke, in the New Testament, Chapter 15.
5. For additional reading on the Prodigal Son story see Henri Nouwen, *The Return of the Prodigal*. (New York: Doubleday, 1992).
6. David Wagner, *Life as a Daymaker*. (Minneapolis: Juu Holdings, 2002), 34.

Chapter 12 – Renew Your Vision

1. Salmon Kahn, *The One World Schoolhouse: Education Reimagined* (London: Hodder & Stoughton, 2012), 179.
2. Edwin H. Friedman, *A Failure of Nerve: Leadership in the Age of the Quick Fix* (New York: Seabury Books, 2007), 32-46
3. Ibid., 53.

Additional reading on Dreaming and Planning:

Beck, Martha. *Finding Your Own North Star*. New York: Three Rivers Press, 2002.

Bregman, Peter. *18 Minutes: Find Your Focus, Master Distraction, and Get the Right Things Done*. New York: Business Plus, 2012.

Covin, Geoffrey. *Talent is Overrated*. New York: Portfolio/Penguin, 2008.

Ellsberg, Michael. *The Education of Millionaires*. New York: Portfolio/Penguin, 2011.

Ferris, Tim. *The 4-Hour Work Week*. New York: Crown Publishers, 2007.

Gladwell, Malcolm. *Blink*. New York: Back Bay Books, 2007.

Gladwell, Malcolm. *Outliers: The Story of Success*. New York: Back Bay Books, 2011.

Gladwell, Malcolm. *The Tipping Point*. New York: Back Bay Books, 2002.

Godin, Seth. *Linchpin*. New York: Portfolio/Penguin, 2010.

Godin, Seth. *The Icarus Deception*. New York: Portfolio/Penguin, 2012.

Godin, Seth. *We Are All Weird*. Irvington: Do You Zoom, 2011.

Pressfield, Steven. *Do the Work*. Irvington: Do You Zoom, 2011.

Pressfield, Steven. *The War of Art*. New York: Black Irish Entertainment, 2012.

Sivers, Derek. *Anything You Want*. Irvington: Do You Zoom, 2011.

Vanderkam, Laura. *What the Most Successful People Do Before Breakfast*. New York: Portfolio/Penguin, 2012.

32029104R00150

Made in the USA
Lexington, KY
06 May 2014